CORE BUSINESS PROGRAM

ORGANIZATION THEORY

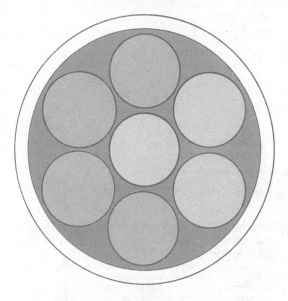

By
P. Bryans
and
T. P. Cronin

Edited by
C. Gilles van Wijk

Facts On File Publications
460 Park Avenue South
New York, N.Y. 10016

CORE BUSINESS PROGRAM
ORGANIZATION THEORY

P. Bryans, BA, MSc(Econ)
T.P. Cronin, BA, MSc(Econ)
Edited by: C. Gilles van Wijk, Ph.D., Dipl. Phys.

Copyright © 1984 by Mike Morris Productions Inc.

Published by Facts On File, Inc.
460 Park Avenue South, New York, N.Y. 10016

First edition published in the United Kingdom in 1983 by
Mitchell Beazley London Ltd., Mill House,
87-89 Shaftesbury Avenue, London W1V 7AD, England.

Library of Congress Cataloging in Publication Data

van Wijk, C. Gilles
Organization theory.

1. Organization. 2. Organizational behavior.
3. Management. I. Title.
HD31.V36 1985   302.3′5   84-8058
ISBN 0-8160-0052-2
Printed and Bound in Great Britain
1 0 9 8 7 6 5 4 3 2 1

Contents

Introduction

This volume on organization theory examines organizations and the environments within which all business activities are pursued. The material covered provides a balanced view of the complexity and diversity of the field. Indeed, the study of organizations entails a knowledge of different theoretical perspectives and their application at different levels in the social system. There is no one best way of doing things inside the organization, hence there are no universal solutions to such problems as effectiveness, leadership or motivation. Every situation is in some ways unique, and only the understanding provided by a careful analysis of the whole situation can lead to appropriate action. This perspective reflects recent developments in organization theory which have led away from earlier positivist research. A useful by-product of contemporary theory is its capacity to incorporate such other subject areas as the decision sciences. The scope and limitations of these specialized domains can be grasped successfully with the insight provided by organization theory.

In particular, this volume develops the implications of two radically different perspectives of organizational life. The traditionally established perspective is structural: organizations are exposed to technological and environmental constraints to which they must adapt. The effectiveness or efficiency or satisfaction of individuals, groups and departments is determined by the organization's formal arrangements. Organizing is then a question of finding the best balance between different preexisting constraints. On the other hand, an increasingly popular perspective is phenomenological: the individual is extensively making sense of his environments. Rather than a unique, objective reality, he is faced with his own interpretations of the context. Everyone's "reality" can thus be different. In order to achieve organized action, it is then necessary to reach a partial consensus as to what is going on, and how it should be interpreted. This "interpretive" view of the organizational reality influences all levels of organized life as the inter-individual processes gradually build up throughout the organization. Clearly, both perspectives contribute substantially to the analysis of social systems. More important, despite their fundamental differences, they do not exclude each other. It is one of the objectives of this book to familiarize the reader with both perspectives.

Chapter 1 examines various approaches to the study of organizations, tracing developments from classical theory in the structural tradition and from social action theory in the phenomenological tradition. Chapter 2 considers the impact of the structural and the phenomenological perspectives on the definition and the analysis of the organization as a whole. Chapter 3 focuses more particularly on the role of structure; the need for various degrees of mutual adjustment provides a rationale for different structural arrangements. Chapter 4 appraises various means used by organizations to control their activities. The increasing importance of computer systems for organization control leads to a discussion of vertical information systems. Management by objectives is also given emphasis as this approach incorporates more participative elements in the control process. Chapter 5 looks at the broader context of organizations, introducing a number of concepts useful in the analysis of the organizational environment and suggesting ways to deal with it. Chapter 6 examines the role of conflict and politics in the organization as well as the means to reduce their disruptive effects. Chapter 7 assesses the role of formal and informal groups for design and performance. Chapter 8 focuses on the nature of perception, the development of attitudes and their consequent effect on behavior. Chapter 9 appraises the complexities surrounding processes of motivation, distinguishing between content and process theories. Chapter 10 concludes with an examination of the function of influence, power and authority in organizations. These concepts provide a background for a discussion of leadership theories.

This book, with its key terms and unique format, will not only be of particular benefit to those studying for MBA degrees, but will also be of great utility to practicing managers.

Chapter 1

Approaches to the Study of Organizations

INTRODUCTION

Organization theory seeks to understand, explain and predict organizational processes both at the individual or "micro" level and at the global or "macro" level. At the micro level it deals with questions of division of labor, motivation, leadership, etc. At the macro level organization theory addresses questions of organizational structure, interorganizational relations and strategic issues, like competitive strategies. In both cases, theory should not be divorced from practice; by providing an understanding of the organizational processes, theory is the basis of management decisions on how to act in given situations.

The study of organizations is characterized by a great variety of approaches with divergent philosophical underpinnings. For instance, the rational and the political framework proceed according to very different lines. The rational view holds that the organization proceeds according to a recurrent pattern involving three basic steps: occurrence of problems, search for alternatives, and choice of the optimal alternative. The political view, on the other hand, proposes that different alternatives can be preferred by different groups, and that the group that prevails will impose its preferences on the others. Both views are important as they provide complementary perspectives. Reliance on a single perspective does not account for the complexity of organizational life. Unlike the physical sciences that are guided by a single paradigm, the study of organizations requires the knowledge of various perspectives. This knowledge leads to practical consequences relevant to the manager, by providing a balanced view of the organizational reality. A manager's understanding of the events will help him to decide upon a future course of action.

Attempts to improve our understanding of human activity in organizations have come from both managerial practitioners and academics representing a wide range of disciplines. Particular groups have emphasized different aspects of organizations, including economic, technical, social, psychological and structural factors. We will summarize here the major developments in theory which will be expanded upon in later chapters.

1. Classical organization theory ⎫
2. Human relations school ⎬ Structuralist tradition
3. Systems theory ⎭
4. Social action theory — Phenomenologist tradition

The above list classifies theoretical developments in their historical sequence.

In the structuralist tradition, the individual "behaves" in response to environmental cues. Differences among individuals are relatively less important. Theorists' attention has been devoted to ways in which the work-environment can be designed, according to scientific rules, to ensure motivation, productivity, satisfaction, etc. In the phenomenologist tradition the individual "acts"; he deals with environmental contingencies and shows initiative. Through exchanges with his co-workers in the organization, the individual develops shared understandings and a shared view of organizational "reality". This "reality" is not objectively given, but is a mixture of material constraints and informal understandings such as group norms. Organization in this perspective is not necessarily achieved by setting rules and procedures; it is much more a **negotiated order** that relies on the coherence of the members of the organization to perform effectively. The next sections of this chapter will follow the development of the principal perspectives from an historical point of view.

CLASSICAL ORGANIZATION THEORY

The systematic concern with organizations as an object of study developed progressively throughout the first half of the twentieth century. The Industrial Revolution produced a proliferation of increasingly complex organizations wherein preoccupation with effectiveness and productivity emerged in response to increasing competition. At that time organizational writers were mostly experienced practitioners seeking new and better ways to manage organizations, focusing particularly on the industrial worker. Many of the concepts and principles that were developed had a lasting influence on organizational thought. The essential theme was to design the organization to maximize its members' performance.

Three major strands can be identified within classical theory – **scientific management, formal organization theory** (sometimes referred to as administrative theory) and **bureaucracy.**

Scientific management owes its origins to Taylor who, rather than create a science of management, produced a number of guidelines for managers to replace the existing "rule of thumb" methods. The ideas of hierarchical structure and division of labor (breaking the production process down into numerous simple tasks) were implicitly recognized, though it was only with the translation of the writings of Weber in the fifties that they gained formal recognition. Taylor focused his attention on how managers could control and coordinate the performance of tasks so as to improve organization efficiency – hence, scientific management is sometimes referred to as task management. The most efficient methods of performing tasks were studied using scientific methods such as time and motion studies and, to induce individuals to adopt these methods, Taylor introduced incentive payment schemes such as payment by results. Organizations could therefore maximize their output levels as efficiently as possible while at the same time workers could increase their earnings levels. It was therefore believed that workers would accept scientific methods since what was good for the company was clearly also to their advantage. In the interests of efficiency, management would also have to pay more careful attention to the selection and training of individuals.

Clearly the mechanistic, economic view of man was one-sided. It failed to take account of how people at work are affected by social variables like informal group behavior. Furthermore, few jobs are suitable for piece-rate incentive plans or payment by results. Often results can be manipulated to meet the requirements set by scientific methods, while the actual labor drops behind. Finally, trade unions questioned the distribution of the gains achieved by increased efficiency.

Scientific management is typically a micro-level approach to organizations with the goal of optimizing performance at the shop-floor level. The other two strands of classical theory, formal organization theory and bureaucracy, are viewed as more of a **macro-approach** – dealing with structure and developing principles applicable to higher authority levels in the organization.

Formal Organization Theory has its origins in the writings of practitioners like Fayol. They propounded that organizations could be managed more efficiently if certain universal principles were applied. These principles provided the guidelines for formal organization structure and included the following:

1. Specialization by function and division of labor – tasks were sub-divided and employees performing those tasks were allocated to functional departments.

2. Scalar principle The chain of command was a line of authority moving downwards through the organization structure.

3. Unity of command The idea of employees having to report to one supervisor.

4. Span of control Determined by the optimum level of effective supervision which, though variable, was considered to be five or six subordinates per supervisor.

5. Vertical communication The chain of command was the official channel for communication.

6. Minimum authority levels Reducing the number of

levels of authority, thus making communication and control
easier and hence improving efficiency.

7. Line and staff division Line departments were to have
direct responsibility for decisions relating to the production
of a good or service, and staff departments, e.g. personnel,
were to provide specialist advice and services to assist the
line departments.

The formal organization theorists overemphasized structure at the expense of sociological and psychological factors
relating to the individual. They shared with scientific management thinkers the model of man as a rational economic
being optimizing his inducement/contribution balance. This
view leads to search for universal keys to problems of organizational structure. Yet these appear not to exist. Other
factors in the organization setting may have an important
influence on structure which they overlooked. For example,
Woodward's work (1965) on how different types of technology (small batch production, mass production, continuous process) might affect organization structure.

Bureaucracy forms the final strand of classical theory. The
bureaucratic model was depicted by Weber, a German
sociologist, as the most appropriate form of organization for
industrial production. The bureaucratic model is based on
the notion of rational legal authority, that is authority which
employees freely recognize as inherent in the manager's
position in the hierarchical structure. Each position in the
organization is defined by a set of rules and procedures
guiding the organizational members' activities. Duties and
rights are predetermined. The amounts of discretion and
authority are strictly controlled at each level. Presumably
the functioning of the organization is independent of any
particular individual provided only that he has the qualifica-
tions to fill the position. Loyalty is fostered by promotional
opportunities along the hierarchical ladder, and is based
purely on merit. The substitutability of employees is
ensured by the existence of written rules and procedures
that are supposed to contain the necessary knowledge for
the adequate performance of the job.

Bureaucracy has many of the characteristics of the other
strands of classical theory: a mechanistic view of man, the
prevalence of hierarchy and authority, and the neglect of
social and psychological influences on the behavior of
people in organizations. Many studies made since Weber
devised his model have highlighted the dysfunctional consequences of bureaucratic organizations. Merton (1940)
showed how compliance with rigid rules and procedures
could become a goal in itself rather than the achievement of
actual organization goals. Most people claim to have
experienced to some degree problems of "red tape" in
bureaucratic structures. Burns and Stalker (1961) did not
question the internal logic of the bureaucratic model, but
rather the goodness of fit of such organizations in changing
economic and social environments. They classified organ-

izations into the broad categories of *mechanistic* and *organic* forms. The rigidity inherent in bureaucratic structures was found to be more appropriate for organizations dealing with recurrent and predictable tasks partly as a consequence of a stable environment; such organizations were classified as mechanistic. In rapidly changing and turbulent environments the organization needs to be more of an organic form: non-routine situations arise continuously and have to be dealt with in an innovative fashion. Instead of enforcing the chain of command in which information and commands move vertically, lateral relations are developed making mutual adjustment more flexible and more rapid.

In their search to improve organization efficiency, classical theorists concentrated on the analysis of tasks and formal organization structure. Human behavior in organizations was seen as being non-problematic. They considered that employees would behave in a rational economic manner and operate within the formal organization structure. The weakness of these theories in explaining human behavior in reality was a gap which the next group of theorists attempted to fill. This major stage in the historical development of theory came from a group of academics in the social sciences who were primarily concerned with the social and psychological influences upon human behavior in organizations.

THE HUMAN RELATIONS SCHOOL

Often considered synonymous with the Human Relations School are the **Hawthorne experiments** carried out by Mayo and associates in the 1920s and 1930s. These experiments examined aspects of the work environment (e.g. length and spacing of rest periods, and physical surroundings) to see how they affected employee productivity. The first experiment examined the effect of varying illumination levels on worker performance. The results were the beginning of a number of puzzling findings. Where output levels were expected to decline they in fact noticeably increased. Experimental methods were then improved upon and other variables thought to influence performance were introduced. A small group of female operators assembling telephone relays was isolated and subjected to extensive observation. Researchers measured performance levels as they changed the working conditions, such as the length of the working day, frequency and length of rest periods, and the quality of lighting. Irrespective of the working conditions, output levels increased. Even after returning to pre-experiment conditions output levels remained high and sickness and absenteeism fell. A further experiment with males in the bank wiring room showed how individual payment schemes were influenced by group relationships and how groups established their own rules on levels of output.

From the earlier experiments it was concluded that output levels were not merely a function of strict supervision levels, incentive payment schemes or physical working conditions, but rather that aspects of the **social system** had to be taken into account. The bank wiring room experiment illustrates the importance of group relationships and group attitudes. In the earlier experiments it can be concluded that it was not so much the change in the physical environment which caused the change in performance levels but the fact that the researchers were showing an interest in the employees subjected to the study. This social effect is sometimes referred to as the **Hawthorne effect**. This group of academics then went on to demonstrate the significance of informal organization structure on the behavior of individuals and work groups which operated alongside, and sometimes in conflict with, the formal organization structure.

Although the Hawthorne experiments have not been without their critics, they do appear to have prompted the beginnings of a theory of human behavior which highlights the social system operating within an organization. Areas such as motivation, morale, democratic leadership styles, interpersonal relations, communications and group dynamics were found to be among the factors influencing productivity and worker satisfaction. The instrumental view of the factory worker was progressively replaced by the awareness that the worker responds effectively to contextual cues, rather than only mechanically. Moreover it was realized that the employee's social needs were rarely satisfied by formal structures. The increasing readiness of management to accept this view led to comprehensive efforts in introducing new methods of management. The emphasis on structure and on the utilization of human resources was replaced by an emphasis on informal activities, and on the factors influencing group formation and group attitudes. This new direction defined by the Human Relations School was thought to achieve better productivity levels and a more satisfied work force.

In the post-war period the Human Relations School was a forerunner of a new school of thinking comprising behavioral scientists and sometimes referred to as the **Neo-Human Relations School**. This included people like Likert (management styles), Argyris (individual well-being), McGregor (employee motivation) and Herzberg (job enrichment), who all developed theories on the relationship between individuals and the organization and who will be considered in greater detail in later chapters of the book.

When taking stock of contributions to organization theory up to the 1950s and 1960s, it can be seen how classical theorists stressed task management and organization structure while the Human Relations School emphasized the social and psychological inflences on human behavior. Other writers were also paying attention to the technological influences on behavior and the economic and social context of organizations – brief mention has already been made of the work of Woodward and Burns and Stalker. The scientific approach of Taylor also formed the basis for a more sophisticated application of science to the management process by operational researchers, economists and management scientists. The problem was one of attempting to find a conceptual framework in which to integrate all these different elements; this became the major objective of systems theory.

SYSTEMS THEORY

The initial attempts to integrate the formal and the informal views of organization were made by a group of researchers from the British Tavistock Institute. Organizations are viewed as socio-technical systems which stress the interrelationship of structural and perceptual factors. Technology, environment, attitudes and organizational structure are all linked and these variables consequently must be taken into account in organizational research. This makes the socio-technical systems approach interdisciplinary: it attempts to integrate knowledge from fields such as psychology, sociology and economics. The neglect of any of these variables would lead to an incomplete picture and to inadequate or suboptimal prescriptions for organizational change.

An experiment which illustrates the application of the socio-technical systems approach is Trist and Bamforth's study (1951) into methods of underground coal cutting. Technical change introduced a mechanized system to the process of coal extraction called the "longwall method" which replaced a group working system. Under the latter system the group allocated the tasks – preparing, cutting and loading – among themselves. The longwall method introduced a shift system whereby each shift specialized in a separate task. Therefore technical change, introducing specialization, cut across well-developed group relationships and work methods. Hence the technical factor may have been optimized but, since the reciprocal effects of such a change on the social factor had been ignored, the expected improved performance levels did not occur.

The application of the systems approach to the *integration* of all factors affecting behavior in organizations was influenced by similar theoretical developments in the physical, biological and social sciences. General systems theorists, however, did not restrict themselves to the social and technological factors operating in the work situation. As has already been mentioned, the organization structure must also be taken into consideration as well as the environment in which the organization operates. Therefore, if an organization is viewed as a system, it is considered to be made up of a number of sub-parts or sub-components, for example, the technical, sociological and structural elements, while at the same time it is also affected by an environmental suprasystem which comprises economic, social, political and technological influences (Figure 1).

The systems view of organizations is dominated by three notions: input (resources), throughput (conversion process) and output (product). In addition, the key assumptions for the systems perspective are that:

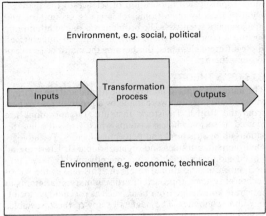

Figure 1. The organization system

1. Organizations have needs for survival

2. Organizations consist of a set of interdependent parts

3. Organizations are behaving and acting entities

Hence the systems perspective offers a conceptual framework in which the organization is analyzed in terms of the functions of its component parts and their mutual interactions. It is important to note that because of the close interrelationships of its components, the organization is more than simply the sum of its constituent parts.

Systems are either closed or open depending on the degree of interaction between the system and its environment. **Closed systems** tend to have rigid, well-defined boundaries which limit interaction with the environment. An organization is generally considered to be an **open system**, having a dynamic relationship with its environment and concerned with the transformation of inputs (e.g. labor and capital) into outputs (goods and services). For the organization to achieve a state of dynamic equilibrium with its environment, continual adjustments have to be made within and between its sub-components.

Systems theory has been criticized for treating the organization as a coherent entity: in this view it can take action, it has needs and it displays a kind of personality in its behavior. This reification of the notion of organization is an inappropriate oversimplification; it ignores the individuals who make up the organization, and its components. In contrast to this, Social Action Theory has presented a radically new approach.

SOCIAL ACTION THEORY

Derived from sociology of work and socio-psychological

Date	Theory	Approach
Pre-1930's	Classical organization theory: (1) Taylor's scientific management (2) Formal organization (3) Weber's bureaucracy	Emphasis on task management (1) and formal organization structure (2 & 3). Developed principles closely linked to hierarchy and authority in organizations. Rational economic view of man.
1930's & 1940's	Hawthorne experiments: Development of Human Relations School	Experiments highlight the social and psychological influences on organization behavior. Emphasis on interpersonal relations, communications, leadership style, motivation, morale. Social view of man.
1950's & 1960's	Neo-human Relations School	Further development of Human Relations School by Behavioral scientists like Likert, McGregor, Herzberg. Self-actualizing man – importance of intrinsically rewarding work.
Late 1960's Mid-1970's	Development of Systems Theory and The Contingency Approach	Organization behavior viewed as the outcome of the interaction of economic, social, psychological, structural, technological variables. Variables describe the organization as a whole. Complex view of man.
Mid-1970's onwards	Application of phenomenological view to organizations: interpretive paradigm	Actor centered approach. Organization is result of set of interlocking behaviors. Organizational "reality" is socially constructed through active processes of sense making.

See Chapter 2 for further explanation of views of man.

Figure 2. Historical development of organization theory

traditions, social action theory views the organization as the outcome of the interaction of motivated people that do not necessarily have an unambiguous "central value system." Not only is the focus brought back on the individual, but the individual is also given the opportunity to "act" autonomously rather than just "behaving," i.e. responding to environmental cues. The context of activities *and* the interactions among members of the organization are the sources of meaning by which actions are interpreted. This **interpretive paradigm** in which meaning is not objective but subjectively ascribed adds a historical dimension to the analysis of the organization and its members: the "sense making" is largely determined by past experience. Sense making is a process everybody engages in, and it is a continuous "sizing up," and modifying of the situation. No situation is therefore ever really given for an individual to behave in; instead by each action it is itself modified. Due to its feedback structure this view of man, and the organizations that it implies, are relatively complex and defy the traditional research and design approaches. The development of the notion of rules has proven useful in this sense to the social action perspective. Formal rules, on the one hand, have an official status by being written or expressed by formal authorities. Informal rules are, on the other hand, more implicit; in addition they cut across the lines of authority. Developed through "ways of doing things" and by ongoing interactions, they establish a temporary social order. They are a complement and sometimes a corrective to formal rules, which frequently fail to deal adequately with non-standard situations. The strict enforcement of formal rules inside the organization illustrates this point by often being counterproductive. In contrast, by allowing processes of mutual adjustment to take place against a background of formal rules and standards, a smooth operation can be achieved. The fact that a "situation" is not objectively given but is continually shaped by the actors is reflected by the term "negotiated order," coined by the so-called Chicago School, a group of sociologists active in the 50's and 60's.

During the study of two psychiatric hospitals, Strauss and others (1963) noted the extent to which all categories of personnel, including doctors, nurses, patients and administrative personnel, were continually negotiating about something. Moreover, formally stated rules were observed to fall into disuse or to be ignored altogether without affecting hospital functioning in any major way. It was argued that traditional approaches to the study of such hospitals had largely underplayed the importance of the observed phenomenon. Though these researches strictly limited their conclusions to psychiatric hospitals, the notion that rules are temporal and that social order is continually being shaped by the organizational members influenced later research.

Fairly recent work in the line of an interpretive approach to the study of organizations, led to the notion of enactment by Weick (1979). The term **enactment** captures the more active role that organizational members are presumed to play in creating the environment in which they live. Furthermore Weick developed the notion of **loose coupling** initially proposed by Simon. According to this hypothesis most of the organization's component parts are loosely coupled with each other; changes in one department will not affect other departments very much or very soon. This provides a degree of stability to the organization as a whole. If there were not an absorbing mechanism like this, the operation of an organization could be upset by the slightest perturbation.

Organizational thinking has substantially progressed by moving away from the structuralist analysis. However, the difficulties generated by social action theory and the interpretive paradigm are multiple. From the practitioner's point of view this perspective does not provide any keys to improved performance or resolution of personnel problems. Only the in-depth study of a particular site by so-called participant observation can lead to the identification of problems and their resolution. From the point of view of the researcher, new methods have to be used like the case study and participant observation. The contribution of the theory should at any rate not be underestimated. By introducing a new way of thinking about organizing, social action theory restores the organizational member to his position of an active and creative being. Furthermore the theory makes it possible to delineate more clearly the extent to which planning, programming and optimizing are possible in the organization and at which points the more unpredictable human factors have to be reckoned with.

SUMMARY

The various approaches to the study of the role of man in organizations have been traced historically (Figure 2). The approaches can be grouped into two broad classes: the structuralist and the phenomenological or interpretive approaches. The structuralist school has dominated research up to the late sixties. It provides mostly explicit prescriptions about how to achieve "performance," "satisfaction," etc. In some aspects the generalizations of the structuralist approach were very successful, while in other domains more sophisticated theories were needed to account for more subtle organizational phenomena. Research methods that entailed closer observation of the processes like case studies had already been advocated by the Human Relations School. With the increasing popularity of the interpretive study of organizations, such methods have been gaining momentum. At this stage the challenge will be for organization theories to fruitfully combine quantitative and qualitative research methods. The contribution to practice is likely to be less prescriptive and more analytical. Managers need the tools to analyze their organizations rather than "universal" prescriptions.

Chapter 2

Complex Organizations – Definitions

INTRODUCTION

Chapter 1 provided various perspectives on the study of organizations. The structuralist perspective emphasized the *goals* to be achieved: effectiveness, satisfaction, performance. The interpretive perspective instead emphasized the *process* by which outcomes can be understood. Accordingly, definitions for the concept of **organization** diverge substantially; "two or more people uniting to coordinate their activities in pursuit of a common set of goals" is structural in highlighting purpose and instrumentality. "An organization is a set of people with mutual understandings and expectations regarding causes and effects of their actions" is an interpretive definition because it underscores the processes by which coordination is ensured. Obviously the two views are valid and must be kept in mind when attempting to understand organizations. To begin with we will consider the structural definition and the logic of organizational goals which follow.

WHY ORGANIZATIONS HAVE GOALS

Most of the following argument, it will be noted, is derived from a systems perspective. Etzioni (1964) defines an organizational goal as "a desired state of affairs which the organization attempts to realize."

A goal or set of goals provide the foundation on which an organization is built. Goals serve a number of purposes:

1. Goals provide a yardstick against which to assess the performance of the organization. Two key performance measurements are often identified – effectiveness and efficiency. **Effectiveness** is a measure of the success of the organization in attaining its goals, while **efficiency** is a measure of how well the organization has utilized its resources in attaining those goals. Efficiency is normally measured in terms of costs or productivity. While organizations which are effective are usually efficient, and vice versa, this may not always be the case. For example, a business organization whose goal is to maximize profits may be ineffective due to a recession in its product market; it may at the same time be efficient in the way it utilizes its resources.

2. Goals establish **guidelines** as to how an organization should function. They lay the foundations for the organization planning process, which is explained in Chapter 4. In large, complex organizations goals tend to be arranged in a hierarchical fashion – the overall organization goal at the top of the hierarchy followed by functional, departmental and individual goals.

3. The establishment and communication of goals may act as a **motivating device** to members within an organization. Individual behavior is seen as goal directed. Hence it is one of the tasks of the structural approach to bring individual goals into line with organizational goals.

Despite the usefulness and the simplicity of **goals** for the understanding of organizations, behavioral scientists have pointed out a number of problems surrounding the identification of organizational goals, partly as a consequence of the system perspective.

THE NATURE AND THE FUNCTION OF GOALS

Goals provide a common denominator to the activities carried on in the organization. Indeed all activity is assumed to be purposive and (generally) profit-maximizing.

A first major problem associated with this unifying function of goals concerns the very question of whether organizations can be said to have any overarching goals. Cyert and March (1963) have argued that organizations as abstract entities do not have goals, rather, it is groups and individuals within organizations who have goals. As already noted, the reification of the abstract notion of organization endows it with quasi human characteristics, e.g., performing actions, taking decisions, and, of course, having goals. As expanded upon later, Cyert and March conclude that organizations have multiple goals which result from the interaction of the major interest groups within them.

The second problem surrounding the identification of organization goals is distinguishing actual goals from stated goals. The two are not always synonymous. When organizations are established there is normally some formal written statement which expresses their goals. However, researchers observing organization behavior question whether these goals are the major determining forces behind organization activity. Perrow (1961) describes these formal goals as **"official goals"** whereas the goals which tend to influence actual behavior in organizations are referred to as **"operative goals"** which are linked directly to the numerous interest groups which make up the organization. Therefore, the study of organization effectiveness requires a closer examination of these operative goals which may or may not be in line with the official goals.

Perrow's classification is similar to that which distinguishes goals as either ends in themselves (official goals) or means to achieving the ends (operative goals). Where an organization's original goals (ends) are effectively substituted by other goals which normally represent the means to achieve the original ends, this is referred to as **goal displacement**. The result is a reversal of ends and means with the latter becoming the goals of the organization. The process of goal displacement was pointed out by Michels in 1911 in his study *Political Parties*, which examined socialist parties and

trade unions in Western Europe. He argued that in those
organizations the maintenance of the organization and the
desire of the leadership to retain office became more important organization ends than the original goals set in accordance with socialist doctrines. By controlling the information and communication networks, officials were able to
retain their positions – a situation Michels described as the
"iron law of oligarchy."

Merton (1940) criticized the operation of bureaucratic
organizations in a similar vein. He claimed that goal displacement could occur in bureaucracies when adherence to
the well-defined rules and procedures of an organization
becomes an end in itself rather than the means of attaining
the goals of an organization.

A final point on goal identification is that goals are influenced by, and may change in response to, **environmental
pressures**. The influence of the environment on organization activity is outlined in Chapter 5. Thompson and
McEwen (1958) argued that organization goal-setting is
influenced by four different forms of interaction with the
environment:

1. Competition with other organizations, e.g. business
organizations competing in product and labor markets.

2. Bargaining between organizations, e.g. collective bargaining between employers and trade unions.

3. Co-optation which involves external organizations being
granted internal influence, e.g. banks providing board directors in business organizations.

4. Coalition formation between two or more organizations.

This first section has emphasized some of the problematic
aspects of goals. The distinction between official goals and
operative goals has underscored the problem of coherence
between what "ought to be," i.e., the organizational objectives, and "what actually is," i.e., the plurality of interests
driving various coalitions within the organization. Finally it
was seen that goals can change as a consequence of
environmental pressures. Goals are thus in no way static;
they vary due to internal and external pressures. In the
following section a widespread assumption will be questioned: to what extent is profit-maximization the business
organization's primary goal?

PROFIT-MAXIMIZATION AND
PUBLIC INTEREST

Various typologies have been proposed for classifying
organizations based on their goals. A simple and widespread classification distinguishes private sector and public
sector organizations. Private sector organizations have presumably profit-maximization as their dominant goal, while

the public sector covers the organizations of central government, local government and agencies. This group of organizations is usually established to meet some general social needs which cannot necessarily be supplied on a normal free enterprise basis.

Hence the objectives of public sector organizations are not directly linked to profit. A certain ambiguity necessarily arises as to the exact mission of service organizations, like hospitals, that have to reconcile conflicting goals by both breaking even and providing adequate services. In most such cases of conflicting goals, measures of effectiveness and efficiency are difficult to derive. Third party payments (e.g., governmental) generally resolve the financial problems, but they do not preclude a cost ineffective operation.

If the goals of public sector organizations are considered ambiguous, the goals of private sector organizations have always been assumed to be linked to the **profit motive**. In contrast to the private sector, the public sector is owned and financed by the State. In the private sector the owners who are the shareholders invest capital in order to reap returns in profits, paid as dividends. (Note that different types of business concerns exist, e.g. sole proprietor, partnership, joint stock company. Readers are referred to another book in this series entitled *Business Economics*.) Such business concerns exist to satisfy consumer demands and if successful the owners are rewarded by profits. This raises the question of whether or not the sole goal of business organizations is, as classical economists assumed, the maximization of profits.

With the growth of large-scale, complex business organizations, it is now apparent that it is an over-simplification to consider the goal of firms in singular profit maximization terms. The classical economic assumption of profit maximization implies that the interests of the firm's owners and managers are identical. This may have been more appropriate where the entrepreneur acted as owner-manager but with the growth of large companies there has been a *divorce of ownership and control*. In modern companies stakeholders as the owners of the company entrust the running of the affairs of the organization to a professional management team. A serious criticism leveled at organization typologies based on goals was expressed by Perrow (1979). In practice, these typologies have not proven useful. The objective is to find typologies that can deal with the variety of organizational forms and help explain differences in structure and goals. Perrow suggests that useful typologies would be based on characteristics that are independent of goals and structure (e.g., tasks) to avoid tautologies: coercive organizations emphasize the enforcement of formal rules. The distinction between "mechanistic" and "organic" organizational arrangements, it will be recalled, is based on differences in task.

SOCIAL RESPONSIBILITY AND STAKEHOLDER THEORY

The growth of large-scale companies (and consumer sophistication) has also led to an awareness of the business organization's **social responsibility**. With the power of controlling and affecting their environment (e.g., legislation, ecology) large companies have been increasingly subjected to public criticism and scrutiny. Goals are modified externally. Attesting to this is the success with which Ralph Nader fought General Motors. As a consequence business organizations have been fairly eager to anticipate criticism and government intervention. Regarding the notion of "corporate social responsibility," it should be noted that the organization is looked upon as a person that would be able to recognize "good" and "bad," i.e., that would have ethics. As is pointed out by Evans (1981), it is individuals, and management in particular, who make the decisions about what is right and what is wrong. The impersonal collective focus is misleading.

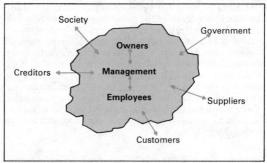

Figure 3. Stakeholder model of the organization

The **Behavioral Theory of the Firm**, developed by Cyert and March (1963) and mentioned earlier in this chapter, sets the basis for a stakeholder perspective on the organization. Cyert and March improve our understanding of why organizations sometimes have multiple goals and how these goals are determined. They view the organization as a coalition of individuals, many of whom belong to an interest group which has its own set of goals. Interest groups in the organization include not only the owners, managers and employees (internal coalition members) but also groups such as customers, suppliers, creditors, government and society in general (external coalition members). All interest groups may influence decision-making within the organization and are sometimes referred to as **stakeholders** (Figure 3).

Each interest group places constraints on managerial decision-making, e.g. customers' demand tastes, government legislation on restrictive practices, employees' desire to obtain favorable wages and conditions, owners' requirements for a satisfactory rate of return. As leaders of organizations, managers have to endeavor to satisfy to some degree the needs of the various interest groups. The presence of diverse interest groups will inevitably lead to goal conflict. Cyert and March argue that the final goal set of the organization results from the *political process of bargaining* between interest groups and as their power may vary over time so may the multiple goals of organizations, e.g. increasing awareness of business organizations' social responsibilities has influenced company policies in the last decade. With many contending interest groups, the achievement of a degree of stability is very important. Cyert and March identify the budget as an important stabilizing mechanism. It is "an explicit elaboration of previous commitments." For the period covered by the budget the expectations are set, and tend not to be questioned until the new budget is up for negotiation. A parallel can be made between the rules discussed in Chapter 1 and this view of goals; both are temporary and negotiated. Furthermore, they serve as guidelines for the action of the members of the organization, resulting in a consistent pattern of interlocked activities.

Having followed the logic of organizational goals to this point, a bridge seems to be found between the structuralist approach and the social action perspective. Quite naturally the following sections will be dealing with the interpretive definitions of complex organizations.

ORGANIZATION PROCESSES

In the same way as goals or outcomes play a key role in the functionalist perspective, processes are emphasized in the interpretive view of organization. The organization is the result of interlocked behaviors, and the successful interlocking is largely achieved by the existence of mutual expectations based on implicit and explicit understandings. Of course this approach provides very much a microview of the processes that take place in organizations. It does not preclude the validity of macroscopic statements such as, for instance, the relationship between size and differentiation (see Chapter 3). Rather, the micro perspective provides alternative **explanations** for the phenomena observed. The following argument, based mostly on Allport's and Weick's work, illustrates how the interpretive approach leads to seeing goals more as a result of the process of organizing them as the initial motivation to getting organized (cf., the functionalist definitions given in the beginning of this chapter).

SHARING RESOURCES VS. SHARING GOALS

The availability of matching resources, e.g., labor, capital and know-how, provides a major impetus for organizing, that is to develop a collective structure with interlocked behaviors of the participants. It should be noted that goals of individuals do not need to be convergent. The fact that the other party possesses the key to the utilization or the

enjoyment of a resource is sufficient to warrant the initial
joining of forces: each benefits the other. Afterwards, to
achieve a degree of stability and predictability in a world of
change, it will be in the partners' interest to maintain their
relationship. As a consequence, through a process of give
and take a broader convergence will develop. A worker can
provide labor, an engineer his expertise, and both will have
notions of what constitutes proper conduct in their regard,
but they generally do not share the goals of a firm until after
they have joined it.

The exchange of means facilitates the accomplishment of
individual designs. This logic provides new insight into
group formation and in particular how the members of the
group *create* social structure. Once the interdependencies
related to interlocking behaviors develop, new goals emerge
that are shared and that subordinate the former diverse
goals. In order for members to continue to enjoy the advantages of the collective structure and the predictability it
ensures, survival of the organization becomes necessary;
survival is a primary component among the newly shared
objectives.

The widespread view that organizations develop on the
basis of common goals probably originates in the process of
causal attribution. People seek valid reasons to explain their
own behavior. In this process they review their interactions,
and these appear most coherent when they are understood
as being motivated by a rational goal. Goals, in other words,
are supplied after the fact, but the initiative develops before
the fact, on the basis of shared means.

By analyzing collective action as a set of interlocking
behaviors that have to be complementary, a radically new
understanding of the development of group structure has
been found. It provides more insight into the dynamics of
organization and into the individual role contributions by
avoiding the reification of abstract notions like, "group" or
"organization."

Two principal criticisms can be leveled at the Social Action
perspective. First, the concern with processes and interlocking behaviors tends to be of limited applicability. The manager is faced with a multiplicity of problems at all levels of
the organization. Yet consequences at the "macro" level are
unclear. Questions about organizational structure remain
mostly unaddressed. The interface between formal rules
and requirements and the informal organizing processes are
not developed.

Second, at the micro level, where the theory is applicable, it
provides only a tool for analysis and understanding, instead
of supplying guidelines for managerial action. Here it could
be argued that guidelines derived from other approaches
have generally not proven universally or consistently valid:
collective structure is continually enacted and can therefore
not be achieved with permanent solutions.

SUMMARY

Two fundamental perspectives on organizations have been developed in some detail. Contrasting definitions have led, respectively, to the discussion of organizational goals and collective action. Goals provide useful guidelines in that they supply a basis for expectations and hence facilitate concerted action. However, goals also appear to be temporary and negotiated. Conversely, concerted action originates in the sharing of resources, while goals develop only afterward through a process of retrospective sense-making. Problems with this approach emerge in assembling the groups in a coherent whole. This question will be addressed in Chapter 3.

Chapter 3

Organization Structures

INTRODUCTION

The primary purpose of organization structure is the creation of a framework that ensures a degree of predictability for the execution of interdependent tasks. With growing size and complexity, organizations tend to develop a number of formal structures aimed at facilitating and rationalizing the work flow. The notion of **division of labor** was an important step towards the structuring of activities; the production process is divided in a sequence of elementary tasks that can be executed by different employees. Together with the concept of **hierarchy**, these notions are basic ingredients for the traditional pyramidal model of organizations. Hierarchy is the system of vertical authority inside the firm. It provides the legitimizing basis for power and control: each role inside the hierarchy is endowed with a certain amount of power. In principle this power is applicable for task-related activities only.

This organizational form met most requirements for efficiency and effectiveness in early industrial organizations. Moreover, with growing output, economies of scale could be achieved by functional specialization. Two factors were, however, to limit straightforward expansion:

1. Material factor: size and diversification resulted in exceedingly complex organizations, in which new solutions had to be found to ensure more efficient management.

2. Human factor: the Hawthorne studies (see Chapter 1) made it clear that interpersonal relations and group processes deserved more attention; labor is not just another resource.

Other related factors could be mentioned that stimulated the research for new organizational forms, e.g., increasing professionalization, complex and turbulent environments, and increasing sophistication of the work force. New developments were introduced both by innovative practitioners and organization theorists. This chapter will present a few important alternative organizational structures, with emphasis on the specific situations they are intended to deal with.

BUREAUCRACY

The most traditional form of organizing is also still the most pervasive, and unlikely to be replaced any time soon. Bureaucracy is characterized by division of labor and a hierarchical structure. The activities inside the bureaucratic organization are closely regulated by formal rules and standard operating procedures. Rules are intended to be **universalistic**, i.e., they apply indifferently to each member of the organization. **Particularistic** rules like favoritism and nepotism violate standards of fairness and can be detrimental to the organization, as they tend to amplify certain traits at the expense of others. The coordination of the production process follows functional lines; related activities are pooled and form functional units. Typical units in a manufacturing company might be production, engineering and sales. The term *function* includes all activities at all levels within each specialization. This basis of organization is known as a functional structure and Figure 4 is an illustration of this type.

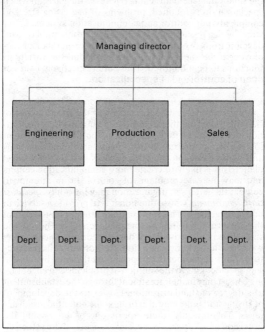

Figure 4. Functional structure

Figure 4 demonstrates a *shallow pyramid* with relatively short chains of command. In reality there may, of course, be other functions depending on size, complexity, product and technology. These may give rise to both *lateral expansion* and an increase in the *number* of scalar levels. Lateral expansion applies in particular to companies with strong staff and technocratic units. These arise as a response to the line function's need for specialized assistance in the management of complex problems and situations. Communication flows must encompass such expansion if these specialist resource areas are to optimize their contribution to the meeting of company objectives. Increasing the number of levels in the scalar chain is often a reaction to organization growth, further specialization and an expanding labor force, reflecting the need for maintaining management control.

In large organizations, structures may also be established on the basis of other forms of grouping, notably by process or by product, where there is considerable diversity in the latter, or by markets. Specialization continues to be the theme around which such structures are created.

In their early stages of development functional structures are usually heavily *centralized*, that is to say major decisions are taken at the top either by the managing director or by the senior management team. Whatever the basis on which specialization is founded, problems of increasing size and complexity put control and communication systems under stress, with a resulting loss of efficiency. Problems of control develop from two main factors, the sheer number of employees to be supervised at each level, and the variety of functions to be monitored. These are respectively issues of **span of control** and of **specialization**.

Extensive research on the span of control has yielded a counter-intuitive result: the narrower the span of control (i.e., the taller the hierarchy) the greater the decentralization (see Chapter 4 for further discussion). The requirement for further specialization may create additional functions and departments on the horizontal as well as the vertical plane. This is likely to create more communication centers and may increase problems of control. In an attempt to combat the latter, an organization may introduce *specialist staff departments* whose function it is to provide a service to line management. This represents an attempt on the part of the organization to relieve line managers of the need to be specialists in all activities. Where this development occurs we have what is known as a **line/staff organization structure**. Staff departments can promote efficiency by harnessing specific skills to the solution of problems and encouraging consistency in their treatment through the establishment of a degree of standardization. However, the development of strong staff units may also bring some potential disadvantages. Theoretically, their role is one of *advice* and the provision of a *support service*, and as such, in theory, they do not possess the authority of office of the line function. Nevertheless, strong staff hierarchies may develop which exercise authority on the basis of the specialized knowledge offered. Their ability to influence the process of decision-making may, consequently, be increased. An ambitious staff department can *exploit* its role, particularly at times when certain of its functions are discharged in an *executive* capacity. When this occurs, the line manager, in accepting service or advice, may be forced into a situation where the decision is in effect being made for him. Typical examples of staff functions are management services, marketing and personnel, although it should be recognized that what constitutes line and staff differentiation will change according to the particular industries to which organizations belong.

Attempts by the organization to maintain control in the face of growth and complexity, and the necessity to involve more and more people, may also take the form of more rigorously applied rules and procedures. This, it is hoped, will result in fewer inconsistencies in decision-making processes, thus avoiding the likelihood of embarrassing precedents occurring. However, tighter controls foster the rigidity of the organization and respecting the rules becomes an end in itself for the members. These dysfunctional consequences have given bureaucracy its image of rigidity. Furthermore, lines of command become stretched, and retention of a high degree of centralized control means that many important decisions are taken at a considerable distance from the point of action. A high degree of centralization may create a situation where top management is attempting to deal with the problems formed by its involvement in both strategic and operational decision-making areas, particularly where the former is neglected in favor of the latter. Controls may come to be seen as ends in themselves, and opportunities for innovation may be diminished and even discouraged. A state of inertia may follow. Briefly, the centralized functional structure experiences two main problems related to expansion:

1. A cumulative loss of control as lines of command lengthen; and
2. The profit-making objective is subtly displaced by operational subgoals.

The need for some form of *decentralization* becomes increasingly apparent when viewed against a background of growth, technological complexity and product specialization. In these circumstances some *reorganization* of structure becomes necessary if the organization is to continue to meet its objectives.

DIVISIONAL STRUCTURES

One solution to the range of problems outlined so far is to build major sections of a business around recognizable and containable divisions. This approach represents a more developed view of functional specialization, and can be achieved on the basis of *product, process* or *markets*, to quote a number of common approaches. An example of a company which has reorganized its structure in this way is shown in Figure 5. Here, the basis for divisionalization is that of *product*.

The *overlaid* pyramid for each division indicates that it can be viewed as a company in miniature, with the role of divisional manager being somewhat akin to that of a managing director. The analogy is not absolute because normally control over important areas of resourcing, notably finance, may be retained by top management, who will continue to exist at the apex of the company structure. **Strategic planning** for the business in total is also likely to be located at this level. However, the whole point of decentralization of this kind is to give each division a considerable measure of *autonomy* in its operations and allow its performance to be assessed separately from other parts of the business. The establishment of **profit centers** based on distinct units of operation allow this process to take place.

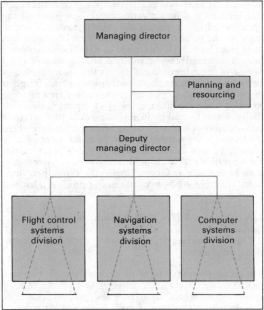

Figure 5. Divisional structure

Based on a comparative historical study of over 70 large US industrial firms, Alfred Chandler (1966) found that organizations did not necessarily adopt the multidivisional structure. Rather, growth strategy determined the choice. Firms engaged in a single industry opted for the centralized structure; other firms pursuing diversification utilized the divisionalized structure.

Divisionalization – some advantages
The multidivisional structure presents a number of characteristic advantages. First, management within each division is given full responsibility for operating decisions. It can develop a degree of expertise that would be unavailable to general management. Each division may have freedom to develop its own markets, drawing on its particular expertise, and may be able to create a response rate to environmental change appropriate to its survival. Second, general management performs only advisory and auditing functions. It can concern itself with **strategic decisions** like long-range planning, resource allocation, appraisal, etc. It is the overall performance of the organization that guides its decisions, rather than less relevant subgoals.

Third, middle management jobs are created worthy of high-caliber personnel. These intermediary management levels are an excellent source of top management candidates.

Divisionalization – some disadvantages

Divisionalization, as with any form of structure, may have drawbacks. Establishing separate divisions within the overall structure can make the concept of a *unified* organization difficult to achieve in practice. There will be a tendency for each division to view its problems in isolation from other parts of the business, and the continuing emphasis on specialization may create problems not dissimilar to those experienced with our simple functional structure. Where financial resources continue to be allocated from the top, conflict may occur between divisions as they compete for funding. Other problems which may arise concern the establishment of priorities between long-term company and short-term divisional objectives, with the management having differing viewpoints on what constitutes reasonable rates of return for each division. It is appropriate to suggest that the organization may aim to achieve a balance between the advantages offered by divisional autonomy and the need to retain an overall sense of perspective, direction and control.

Despite the advantages offered by divisionalization, it may be felt desirable for certain functions to be centralized, notably production, in order to achieve economies of scale. For example, each division can be given freedom to negotiate prices with the organization's own production function, or, if the latter is unable to offer competitive prices, to take its business elsewhere.

In short the benefits of the multidivisional structure clearly appear to exceed the disadvantages, at least for diversified companies.

ALTERNATIVE APPROACHES

Both the functional and divisional models provide a global perspective on the structuring of organizations. Yet they do not necessarily resolve a number of particular problems. For instance specialization and its necessary complement, integration, are separated in the hierarchical structure. However, they may sometimes need to be combined as closely as possible, as is suggested by the results of Burns and Stalker (see Chapter 1). Environmental conditions, or even the technological complexity of a product, require different structures. Further, the functional specialization present in the unitary form as well as in the multidivisional form of organization creates monotonous and repetitive working conditions for a large number of employees. Diversification of the tasks on the other hand requires at least a partial reorganization. What may be required is an organization which allows complexities surrounding the use of modern technology to be handled efficiently, and which achieves a social structure compatible with this aim. If this can be attained we may have an organization which is both economically efficient and socially effective.

The following sections will provide some answers by analyzing the organization in the **information processing** perspective. The purpose is to depict organizations as information processing networks whose principal task it is to **reduce uncertainty**. Uncertainty in the organization stems from the unpredictability of internal and external variation, as well as from complexity. For example, it was mentioned previously how bureaucratic rules were intended to increase predictability, i.e. reduce uncertainty. The information processing perspective resolves mostly logistical problems by focusing on structural arrangements to optimize communication. If there are human needs for variety and task diversification, they require instead an actor centered approach.

LATERAL COMMUNICATIONS AND THE MATRIX STRUCTURE

Focusing on the task as a whole rather than on its component parts it is clear that it entails many **interdependencies**. Various classifications have been proposed for this important notion; Thompson (1967) suggested to distinguish *pooled, sequential* and *reciprocal* interdependencies in the work flow (Figure 6). In pooled interdependence each part makes an independent contribution to the whole; divisions in a multidivisional organization are generally in pooled interdependence with the company. Sequential interdependence presents a more crucial relationship: the interdependence is asymmetric, one part depends on another. For example, distribution depends on production and assembly on fabrication. The third kind of interdependence, reciprocal, is present when component parts require each other's output as their input. This relationship can be found for example between an R & D department and a marketing department. The needs for mutual adjustment are most important for the reciprocal interdependence while they are smallest for pooled interdependence. In order to provide for the necessary volume of communication, functional departments in a pure hierarchy would be adequate only for the pooled situation. Sequential and reciprocal interdependence are likely to require a greater communication capacity than the one provided through the vertical chain of command; in principle, informations and problems flow up and commands flow down. In normal operating conditions these channels would be quickly saturated. Hence **lateral relations** are in order. Various devices exist that permit mutual adjustment to take place across departments while remaining at the same organizational level: liaison roles, task forces, etc. (Galbraith 1977). Opening the lateral channels has the advantage of ensuring faster and better communication among departments, and of alleviating the vertical flow of information.

Still the complexity of certain projects may find the increased information processing capacity insufficient. The

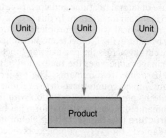

Pooled interdependence

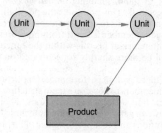

Sequential interdependence

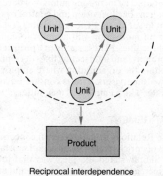

Reciprocal interdependence

Figure 6. Three classes of interdependence

combined use of lateral relations and upward referral is not
adequate to maintain integration. In this case project teams
can be set up to deal with the problem of coordination.
Temporary by nature, the project teams introduce new lines
of authority cutting across the pre-existing functional lines;
a project manager supervises the realization of the project
with all its particular requirements. The project manager
will negotiate with his counterparts in the various functional
areas. Due to its particular configuration with intersecting
lines of command, this organizational form has been named
a **matrix structure** (see Figure 7). This elaborate structure
is most adapted for very complex projects; it was
implemented first by companies such as NASA for its space
programs. The matrix structure is not only applicable to the
management of projects; it can also be formed for geo-
graphical regions, large customers, etc. The example illustrated in Figure 7 takes the case of an engineering project.

The introduction of **project teams** allows greater emphasis
on the task in hand, enabling *improved communication*
between specialists. This promotes the possibility of earlier
and optimum solutions to complex technical problems. The
individual team member is freed from pressures surrounding the maintenance of his role within the function, and his
loyalties will be more sharply concentrated on the project
itself. This in turn may lead to enhanced commitment and
consequent high levels of performance. Opportunity may be
created for members to develop a team structure with strong
psychological and sociological affiliations. There is a relationship between early identification of technical problems,
deriving solutions and cost performance. The project is less
likely to reach the production stage in a state which suggests
a degree of underdevelopment. For example, losses due to
scrap may be minimized, and contract deadlines will not be
affected by the emergence of sudden unexpected problems.

These structural solutions to the organization's coordination problems present a number of difficulties in their
implementation. The increasing amount of decentralization
creates problems of supervision and control by augmenting
discretion at lower levels. (The next chapter on control and
the chapter on motivation will attempt to come to terms
with these difficulties.) The creation of a project team brings
in a new hierarchy, and intersecting lines of command create
positions within the organization where employees have to
report to two supervisors. This is considered as a stressful
situation under which employees may suffer.

JOB ENLARGEMENT

The Human Relations School has been concerned with the
possibilities of enrichment of the task and satisfaction of the
employee. Simply stated the idea was that **job enlargement**, i.e., increasing the variety of tasks, and **satisfaction**
would somehow lead to increased productivity by affecting
motivation. Hence this approach has addressed questions of
structure in a different light. One such experiment has been

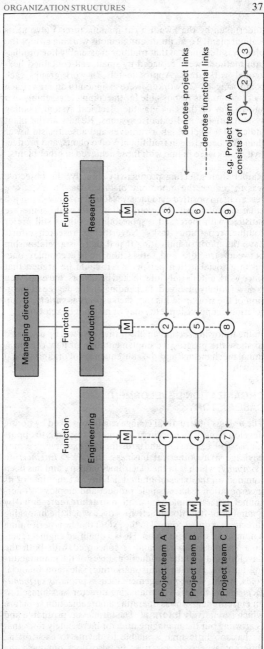

Figure 7. Project/matrix structure

undertaken by the Swedish car manufacturer Volvo at its Kalmar plant. To facilitate autonomous working groups the plant was designed so that traditional assembly line production methods were replaced by small, self-contained hexagonal work areas. Approximately 28 work groups each comprising 15–20 workers were assigned to an area. Each work group was responsible for the complete assembly of a sub-system of the car, e.g. the electrical system, cooling system, engine and exhaust systems. Results at the plant indicated a level of labor turnover and absenteeism lower than that occurring in traditional Volvo plants, and productivity rates were in line with those achieved in other plants.

Rather than affecting productivity directly, the objective was to reduce the monotony of tasks. Despite extensive research, no positive evidence was found to support the job enlargement thesis. Workers differ, and while some are satisfied with increased responsibilities, others still prefer routine, repetitive tasks. Nevertheless research efforts have the merit of indicating that if there is a relationship between structure and satisfaction, it is a complex one. From a social action perspective it could be argued that since work entails only interlocked behaviors, the employee is never totally involved. Depending on the degree of inclusion of the worker in his job, such aspects as variety, group relations, supervision, etc., may or may not be relevant.

In the following section an illustrative case will be discussed to show the progressive implementation of new organizational mechanisms, and the consequences of organizational growth.

ORGANIZATION DEVELOPMENT CASE HISTORY

The *process* of structural change can be observed by noting developments which occur as a company responds to opportunities for expansion and growth. For example, we may envisage a hypothetical business, the *XYZ Engineering Company*, which is in the electronics industry and has been founded on the basis of limited liability. At the time of its incorporation it has a single product and employs 40 personnel. It has a simple organization structure represented by a number of **functional** activities over which the managing director has direct control to the extent that he is performing a number of different **roles**. He is a qualified engineer, acts in a technical capacity and is concerned with both the development and the production stages of the manufacturing process. He also fulfils marketing, sales and financial roles. At this stage, management focus is primarily on *manufacturing and sales*. The managing director sees himself as an entrepreneur who is operating an organization structure which is relatively **informal**. The business is profitable and is growing but the managing director increasingly finds that he has too little time available to devote to each of the different aspects of his role; he also does not have the required degree of specialized knowledge in each sphere.

He finds that much of his time is taken up by having to deal with day-to-day problems which leaves little time for planning the company's future.

Eventually he bows to the inevitable and recruits additional **specialist** staff to head each major function. This move enables him to spend more time in **strategic** and **planning** activities. The newly appointed functional heads report directly to him. At this stage of development **span of control** is not a major problem and there appears to be no requirement for a further level of management. Thus we have a **functional** organization structure which strongly emphasizes *line* departments. However, the business continues to expand and now employs 400 personnel. The range of products continues to increase as new market opportunities present themselves. Line functions and departments require additional specialist assistance in the form of various *management services*. For example, work study and production planning are now of sufficient importance to warrant their establishment on a departmental basis. Personnel problems are of a particular nature and level to justify the **centralization** of policy and practice by the establishment of a personnel function. The managing director finds that his span of control has become too large and that it is now necessary to provide a further level of management between himself and his functional heads. He achieves this by appointing a general manager to whom functional heads will now report. **Communication** and **control systems** are becoming more complex, involving more and more people. Management focus is shifting away from total concentration on manufacturing and sales and there is increasing concern with **efficiency of operations**. Basically, the structure is functional. Yet despite the increase in managerial posts major decisions continue to be taken by the managing director. It is a centralized structure based on direction from the top with limited **delegation** of authority to those below. Changes in structure are paralleled by changes in the relative importance of control systems. Efficiency is increasingly viewed as achievable by the establishment of **rules, procedures** and **standards**. Particular attention is given to **cost control** and to the implementation of mechanisms which enable this to be achieved. The company continues to grow in an expanding market. The product-range is extended with each product-line fulfilling the requirements of a highly specialized market where *technological innovation* is of utmost importance. Considerable attention must now be given to the specialized requirement of each market and it becomes more and more difficult to maintain effective centralized control. The company is experiencing considerable delays in reaching decisions because the process is too slow to cope with the quick response which is required if new market opportunities are to be realized. Employment levels are rising as a result of expanding production and lines of communication become more complex and extended. These lines have now to encompass lateral expansion brought about by the development of large *technocratic and staff units*. Traditional line **authority** is under challenge by the need to respond to authority of a different order, namely that based on technical knowledge. In an attempt to resolve these problems the company decides to reorganize on a **product structure** basis. This approach enables concentration of specialist resources around the design, development, production and sales functions in each main product area. Inevitably, this involves further **decentralization** and delegation of authority.

A product structure will often lead to the adoption of a **divisional structure**, and the company decides to adopt this format. Divisional structure may be considered as an extension of a product-based structure but with additional delegation of authority and autonomy. Each division, based on product specialization, is established as a **profit center** the manager of which is **accountable** to top management for producing an acceptable return on capital. Control systems will now be developed to enable the profit center concept to be maintained. The company will experience an increase in the number of items covered by its management information systems and these are likely to become increasingly sophisticated in their application. Each divisional manager has considerable **autonomy** in relation to the activities of his division. It must be stressed that the adoption of a divisional structure is a reflection of growth in *size* and *complexity*, and the necessity to cope with and respond to rapid environmental change. Each division can respond in its own particular way to the needs of its unique market. The role of top management will have changed significantly during the years of expansion and structural reorganization.

The company has now attained a size where it is employing 4000 personnel and is more than maintaining its foothold in a high technology and highly competitive industry. A number of its product divisions are gaining world-wide recognition in their particular fields. However, the days of reorganization are not yet over. The technology is moving towards a **systems basis** where related items are designed and produced to provide a complete package for the customer. Much of the equipment is computer-based, involving sensor, process and output equipment. The engineering is complex and demands close cooperation between various engineering specialists from the design to the production stages. The divisional structure allows recognition of the particular specializations but it will still have retained many of the features of functional specialization, with each engineering department representing its own hierarchy. This structure finds itself increasingly unable to cope with the required levels of communication and cooperation between departments and between individuals, and failure to achieve this communication and cooperation is likely to result in the occurrence of costly errors. Problems are not being identified at a sufficiently early stage with a consequent misuse of expensive resources.

In order to facilitate a solution to these and other problems the company decides to organize its resources around a series of **projects**. Personnel are drawn from each function and department as required and formed into **project teams**. The functional hierarchies remain but much of their authority has now passed to the project teams. Within each team the various specialists work closely together with the accent on participative decision-making as the means whereby optimum technical and cost-solutions to problems will be achieved. The company has arrived at a point where it has adopted a **matrix structure**. It reflects a management focus which is concerned with the requirements of problem solving and innovation. It stresses the requirement for effective liaison not only between the various technical specialists but in terms of personnel throughout the organization. Over a period of time structural changes have taken place for very definite and sound reasons. Increasing size, growing complexity and the need to maintain efficiency reflect the more prominent influences.

SUMMARY

The purpose of this chapter has been to outline structural considerations. Different structural features enable organizations to choose what is most appropriate to their needs. There is no one best structure suitable for all situations. Increasingly, organizations operate in complex, competitive and rapidly changing environments, and from time to time the need for structural modifications will arise as the organization struggles to adapt to new circumstances. It should be remembered that structure is but one component of an organization. As such it must achieve compatibility with other components, notably control mechanisms, the technology used and the objectives set, if the criteria of efficiency and effectiveness are to be met.

Chapter 4

Organization Control

INTRODUCTION

In its most conventional structural form, control is manifested by rules that direct behavior to ensure coordination and effectiveness within the organization. It is important to note, however, that the activation of rules and explicit commands are but a small part of the coordinating devices. As was pointed out by March and Simon (1958) there are a large number of **latent** means of control that have often been neglected in the analysis of organizations. Examples are programmed tasks, standardization of materials, and standard operating procedures. Much of organizational behavior is shaped by these unobtrusive control mechanisms. They set the premises for most operating decisions and hence contribute to the decentralization of decision-making. Further delegation economizes on managerial decision-making and ensures that decisions are made by a person who is closer to the issue and therefore likely to be more knowledgeable.

Together, the direct forms of control and the unobtrusive forms account for a good deal of the coordination going on in the organization. Nevertheless, a number of questions arise that are diffuse to the point that they can hardly be formulated except in very general terms; in such cases decision-making does not flow up the hierarchy in the normal way. Yet these questions are extremely important to the smooth operation of the organization, even though they are not as immediately visible as other discrete issues. The questions can involve, for instance, the little extra effort needed to do things right. By being unprescribed, they are largely at the discretion of each employee. Control and monitoring cannot really deal with this order of issues, unless it is in the indirect way of an **internalized code**. In the same way that this kind of question is diffuse, such a code entails unspecified commitments that can apply to any situation. With varying degrees of intensity, such codes can work in favor, or against, the collective interests, thus ranging from rampant sabotage to total commitment.

In sum, forms of control can be organized in three separate classes: direct, latent, and internalized. These three classes match up with three kinds of issues: "unique," "standardizable," and "diffuse." Figure 8 presents an overview and indicates how specificity of the form of control is associated with degree of internalization.

CONTROL – SOME CONSIDERATIONS

The various ways of achieving coordination and the use of particular control mechanisms will depend on the nature of the organization's objectives, its organization and management structures, technology and its cultural norms.

Form of control	Direct	Latent	Internalized
Nature of issue	Unique	Standardizable	Diffuse
Specificity of applicable rule	High $-\ -\ -\ -\ -\ -\ -\ -\to$ Low		
Example	Command	Std. procedure	Code

Figure 8. Form of control matched with nature of issue

Control would be simplified if it could be assumed that everyone within the organization had similar objectives, or that its various processes were self-regulating. In practice this does not occur. In the case of individual motives, objectives and behavior have to be considered as much a *reality* of organization life as those which are counted part of the organization's formal goals. The individual represents his own unique position within the overall hierarchy of organization membership and is infuenced by his own ambitions and perceptions surrounding his role. He is also affected by events and experiences *outside* the work place and these may condition his response to the work situation. We cannot even assume that management in its *corporate sense* always acts in such a way as to suggest a *unified* view of organization objectives. The individual manager may view his *specific* departmental objectives as being more important or significant than some more generally stated overall objectives. He may feel that the former serve his own ends more adequately in that they are felt to be more pertinent to the realization of his own goals.

In the structuralist view of March and Simon these problems can be overcome to a large extent by controlling the **premises** of decision. There is an internalized selection process that determines the *relevant information* for a particular decision and there is a limited search process for *acceptable alternatives*. The internalization of premises comes about through learning. For example, early recruitment and lifelong employment is practiced in most Japanese organizations and is typically associated with an almost total involvement of the individual in his organization. Highly selective recruitment is another way of achieving the desirable homogeneity among professional employees, for instance. The control of premises is most important when process and outcomes are hard to monitor and evaluate; it will be more important in the upper levels of the hierarchy.

Direct supervision will be easier and more readily accepted in the lower levels.

CONTROL METHODS

When considering the various methods of explicit organization control we can distinguish between:

1. The use of formal authority.
2. Control through standardization.

Formal authority This has its origins in classical organization theory, and in bureaucracy in particular, and is based on

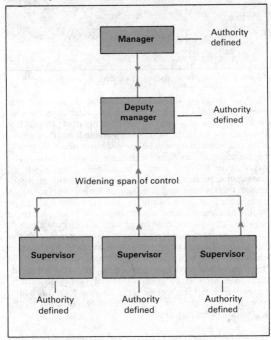

Figure 9. Chain of command – span of control

the notion of *voluntary acceptance of legitimate authority*, and therefore of orders, directives, and requests. In practice this entails supervision achieved through the application of principles relating to *identification* of authority at each level of the organization, and the *establishment* of a chain of command and spans of control. Thus, one level of office carries with it authority and responsibility over the one beneath it (Figure 9). Often, the exercise of this form of control will involve the manager in directing, assessing and correcting actions related to his subordinate's work performance and general behavior. In turn he will be subject to the same process by his superior, and so on up the chain of command. In the business organization *legitimacy arises out of the office* or level of job rather than as a factor relating to the personality of the job holder. This provides the organization with some stability, even when it is faced with sudden changes in staff, and helps to minimize disruption to the process of meeting objectives.

In large and complex organizations this process of control can be complicated by the existence of a number of chains of command affecting the role of the individual. A subordinate may be required to report to two different supervisors for different aspects of his job. If control involving the use of formal authority is to be effective, careful consideration needs to be given to ensure that the divisions of task content, responsibility and reporting relationships are fully *understood* by both supervisors and subordinates (Figure 10).

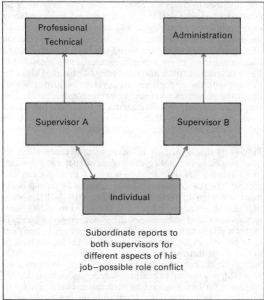

Figure 10. Dual authority structure

Formal authority as a means of control exists in another sense which does not rest on the superior authority inherent in one job as compared to another, but arises because managerial jobs at the different levels of the organization carry with them certain *requirements* and *rights* relating to access, consultation and negotiation with others in the management hierarchy, particularly those in peer relationships. **Lateral communications** of this nature may be necessary to the successful discharge of responsibility and serve as a means of control by establishing a system of checks and balances. For example, the marketing manager in an organization may need to meet with and advise the sales manager. One does not necessarily have right of supervision over the cther, but the *process of consultation* which ensues may serve as an important *restraint* on either manager doing exactly as he pleases regardless of any other consideration. Each person in this type of transaction is recognizing authority in the other's role and may *modify* his own preferences in favor of reaching agreement.

Standardization may take a number of different forms. The standardization of a number of recurrent decisions is extremely important as a means of control. It relieves the decision maker, worker, supervisor or manager from having to make a considerable number of operating decisions from scratch. In addition it ensures predictability and hence facilitates coordination. For instance, two managers within the same organization but operating in different departments and possibly in different physical locations may each be faced with a similar problem. Each manager, independently of the other, may investigate and analyze the problem and then apply the appropriate rule or procedure to the solution of his problem. Both problems and solutions are similar, and thus, consistency of treatment is assured, enabling *stability*. The existence of **rules** and **procedures** also provides employees with the opportunity to develop their understanding of the processes whereby problems are dealt with. The employee may feel that consistency in treatment provides a more *equitable* basis than decisions based on one individual's interpretation of events or facts.

However, this approach to management control has its weaknesses in that too great a dependency on rules and procedures is likely to lead to a *loss* of management discretion. The rule or procedure may come to be seen as being more important in itself than the problem to which it is being applied. In situations where this is carried to excess, allegations associated with some of the disadvantages of bureaucracy are likely to arise, notably that the means to the ends have become more important than the ends themselves. In practice it is difficult to provide a rule or procedure which will cover precisely every problem that is likely to be encountered. Moves toward organization decentralization, with its emphasis on less mechanistic structures, make control of this sort less appropriate. **Flexibility** in the handling of problems is important, as was noted before, especially under such unpredictable circumstances as highly competitive markets, new technologies and irregular supply of resources. Many managerial jobs require exercise of a considerable measure of *discretion* if they are to be effective.

Overall, *excessive* emphasis on the use of formal authority, whether of a direct supervisory nature or through the application of rules and procedures, is likely to provoke reaction on the part of the employee and encourage the development of attitudes and behavior which will result in jobs being performed at minimum standard. Motivation may be poor and the individual's realization of making a useful and meaningful contribution will be low. Cooperation and creativity may well be lost to the organization as a result.

Despite the shortcomings of excessive emphasis on rules, direct and unobtrusive control is a necessary complement to decision-making discretion at all levels of the organizational hierarchy. By dealing with the more routine aspects of the activity, time is available for more substantive decisions. Problems associated with *de novo* decisions are **diffusion** and **implementation**. The costs of informing all those affected by a new decision and having them buy into its implementation are substantial; hence the importance of rules.

A common example is the standardization of **work methods**. They are standardized in such a way as to ensure *consistency* in manufacturing processes and thus in the product. This form of control can be applied at the level of the department, the work group or the individual. Figure 11 indicates various areas where work standards can be established.

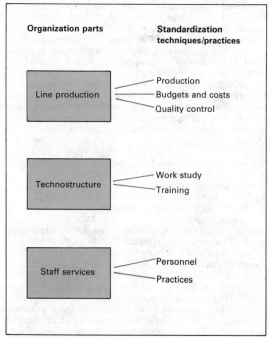

Figure 11. Examples of standardization

Work standardization has become particularly important in manufacturing industry. In part it removes the need for constant direct supervision, replacing it with an authority based on the design, planning and implementation of **technical standards**, adherence to which provides the required degree of control. In effect, **technical authority** is more

relevant to the needs of the organization than formal management authority exercised through direction. Here, we
have used the production process as our example but standardization is often used to control the work of other functions. **Financial control** through the establishment of
budgets and monitoring of costs is one such example. **Management training** aimed at standardizing behavior is yet
another.

CONTROL AND PLANNING

Associated with control is the process of **planning**. Planning involves all levels of the organization even though its
impetus may stem from top management. **Corporate planning** requires identification of the company's *overall*
strategy and the range of measures needed to be taken to
enable realization. The *translation* of strategy into a series of
plans eventually results in the setting of functional, departmental and individual *objectives*. However, before this stage
is attained the strategy itself must be determined. Primarily,
this arises through an examination of both *external* and
internal environments. For example, assessment of the
external environment is likely to include market opportunity, the state of technology, government policy and availability of capital and labor. Assessment of the internal environment requires the organization to take a considered view of
its strengths and weaknesses in relation to existing
resources, competence and so on. Both processes will create
information which may then be used to determine business
objectives and appropriate product development and manufacture. Generally, the questions needed to be asked
include:

1. What position is the organization in at the present time?
2. What are its objectives for the future?
3. What products or services are to be provided?
4. What will constitute an acceptable level of profits?
5. What are its social responsibilities?

The process of translating strategy into plans characterizes
much of the American approach to management and control. It entails determining priorities, setting objectives,
monitoring performance, etc.; all illustrate an explicit use of
control. In contrast, Japanese management can be characterized by its emphasis on ideology and values (Ouchi
1981). Objectives are much more diffuse; a manager does
not get evaluated on the basis of capacity to meet objectives
but on his ability to manage respecting norms and values of
how business ought to be conducted. Instead of *compliance
through control* the Japanese approach emphasizes
informed initiative on the basis of organizational culture.

As business plans are broken down into objectives they
usually become more detailed, and at lower levels may
appear as little more than a set of instructions with limited or
no discretion rather than as a statement of objectives. In
effect chain and unity of command principles are being

employed so that objectives met at one level help to fulfil objectives at the next level above and so on until the plans are realized, and the organization's strategy is eventually discharged.

Clearly, successful control will be subject to the adequacy of organization strategy. For example, if, initially, the organization places the wrong *interpretation* on what is happening in the environment, then however successful the ensuing control process is, it will not compensate for the strategy having been poorly founded.

VERTICAL INFORMATION SYSTEMS

Complementary to the decentralization of decisions, vertical information channels can increase the information processing capacity of the organization (Galbraith 1979). The introduction of computer systems in the workplace provides the opportunity to reduce the decision load moving up the hierarchy while preserving direct or obtrusive control. The constraints placed on the decision process by such information systems is that the information flow has to be standardized and that the alternatives considered are inherently limited by the scope of the input data. A global data basis requires systems of a high capacity and rather complex decision models. A local data basis is easier to deal with but leads to suboptimization which, due to interaction effects, does not necessarily provide globally optimal solutions. However, information systems are efficient in providing **feedback**.

Feedback is an important component of the monitoring process in situations in which formal authority is being exercised. In this instance it is *reaction* to the outcome of particular decisions which provides the feedback – in other words, the *consequences* of that decision in the form of information. Are the consequences the expected ones or by their very nature could they not have been anticipated? What effect will this have on future decisions if and when a similar problem arises? Similar considerations apply to the application of formal rules and procedures, and the extent to which consequences resulting from the implementation of a rule or procedure *reinforce* management's belief in the *validity* of the latter or bring about the desire for change. Figure 12 illustrates how feedback matches each step in the unfolding decision process. Basically, feedback serves to remind us of the dynamic and ongoing nature of organization life, where strategy, plans, objectives and goals are subject to constant *reformulation*. It represents an essential link between the processes of communication; without feedback adequate control would be impossible.

MANAGEMENT BY OBJECTIVES

A major feature of traditional authority systems is that they are *imposed* by managers or by the organization, and thereby reflect particular values. Essentially, they provide a process whereby participation on the part of the subordinate is *minimized*. The individual is expected either to respond to control in a manner favorable to the meeting of formal objectives or suffer the consequences. However, in practice the employee may find some way of rejecting the imposition of authority, for example, by withdrawing cooperation.

Alternative approaches are possible and one of the best known is that of **Management by Objectives** (M.B.O.). The essential feature here involves a process of establishing job objectives based on *mutual agreement* between manager and subordinate. One aspect of this approach is that a system of staff appraisal, based on performance factors related directly to the job, is frequently employed. It is claimed that a subordinate's involvement becomes more substantial and a situation is created in which he will work harder and more effectively. Because he has been encouraged to be the mainspring of his own objectives, his attitudes

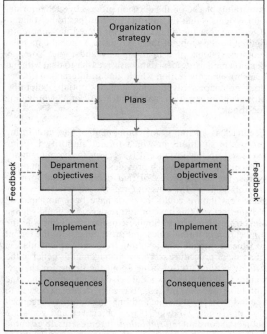

Figure 12. Feedback system

and behavior will demonstrate greater commitment to the overall goals of the organization. Faced with inevitable hierarchical structures, organizations are concerned to make them work effectively. This entails control, but M.B.O. attempts to provide an approach which increases the likelihood of achieving teamwork based on *mutual con-*

sensus as regards goals, and identification of what is expected of the individual. Both manager and subordinate will understand the level of job performance which is expected and will be working within a clearly defined framework. Consequently the possibility of uncertainty surrounding both individual and organization objectives will be removed and, if the process is implemented throughout, should result in the development of a more supportive climate which will enhance the quality of relationships within an organization.

It is also claimed that high levels of involvement on the part of employees will assist the process of *evaluating performance*. M.B.O. requires a measure of self-appraisal on the part of the individual and there is some evidence to suggest that weaknesses are viewed more objectively, possibly because a greater feeling of security exists; in turn this may enable a situation where corrective action is more acceptable. Furthermore, emphasis on the achievement of results may remove some of the doubts surrounding traditional staff appraisal because there is less opportunity for subjectivity to creep into assessments. It is actual **achievement** which is emphasized. M.B.O. is intended to appeal to the individual's desire for *involvement, creativity* and *autonomy*. As with other forms of control, M.B.O. makes assumptions about the nature of the relationship between the individual and his job; McGregor's Theory Y provides some insights into the basis of such assumptions. It proposes a view of man which suggests that he possesses potential for development, is not inherently lazy and will not shirk responsibility and that what is needed is a management approach that encourages the emergence of more positive human characteristics.

Problems can arise with Theory Y because its assumptions about human motivation imply a *general theory approach* which cannot be supported on the basis of existing evidence. Some people are motivated in the manner desired while others, victims perhaps of more traditional approaches to the exercise of control, cannot wholly remove suspicion from their minds that M.B.O. still represents authoritarianism – albeit in a disguised form – and is really a form of **pseudoparticipation**. Opponents of M.B.O. argue that despite its claims, it does not overcome the reward/punishment psychology underlying hierarchical relationships: the *implied threat* continues to be present ready to be invoked in the case of failure. They question the reality surrounding the involvement of the subordinate in the objective setting process, arguing that actual choice of goals is in fact limited by the manager who will continue to be the final arbiter of what is allowable. Alternatively, M.B.O. can be seen as a set of shared objectives that represent a mutual understanding of what ought to be done. Realization of the objective is contingent upon the adherence to accepted rules; breaking the rules implicitly gives the other party the rights to withdraw from its previous commitments. Hence in this social action interpretation, there is no need for broad assumptions regarding human nature. A further problem is that over-

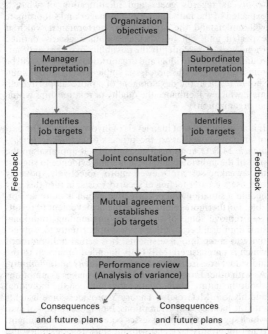

Figure 13. Management by objectives. Annual or six-monthly cycle

dependence on the use of job descriptions may result in too narrow a view on what constitutes acceptable objectives. For example, there are some aspects of a manager's job which are difficult to describe meaningfully, let alone quantify as part of the objective setting process. *Relationships with other managers* may comprise an important dimension and influence how well the individual manager performs, and yet this may be overlooked in the quest for measurable data. Figure 13 illustrates M.B.O. processes.

INFORMAL RELATIONSHIPS

The discussions so far have centered around formal control related to formal organization objectives. However, it is necessary to make some comment on the existence of **informal relationships** and the extent to which they comprise a form of control system. The **Human Relations View** of the informal organization tends to focus on the organization itself as an identifiable entity with its own social structure, communication and status systems. However, more recent studies, notably Silverman's *Theory of Organizations* (1970), suggest that this separatist view is not a wholly accurate reflection of how the total system works, and that formal and informal organizations are really interdependent. Undoubtedly, we can point to the existence of informal communication networks which reflect information flow based on mutual interests and a desire to see those interests realized. Such networks embrace personnel at all levels of the organization, including managers, and supplement communication flows arising out of formal channels of control. They enable the organization to function, as well as reflecting the social nature of life within the organization. In practice, the informal channels provide links between those with shared interests and thus enable powerful pressure groups to be formed (Figure 14).

Formal control systems have to exist alongside pressure groups and acknowledge their existence. Constant readjustment based on the dual processes of negotiation and consultation is likely to be demanded, and can assist the organization to maintain its health and stability. Conflict is most likely to occur when the existence of informal channels and the role they play are denied. Indeed the mutual agreements accumulated during interactions then comes up for

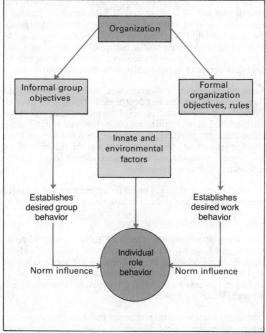

Figure 14. Formal and informal influences on individuals

renegotiation in an abrupt way. As a result, new, informal rules develop restructuring collective action. The progressive adoption of a new order can be seen as the development of new coalitions of interest, that complement and enhance the formal order by filling in the blanks.

Chapter 5

Environment and Organization

INTRODUCTION

The discussion of complex organizations to this point may give the impression that organizational problems and solutions arise only from within. Yet the environment is an important source of problems, and provides at the same time many opportunities to facilitate survival and performance. Various approaches have been suggested to describe analytically the relationship of the organization to its environment. Systems theory and contingency theory provide rather deterministic views. The organization has to fit into its environment if it is to survive. The systems perspective views the organization as embedded in a larger system in which it has to perform functions, e.g., ensure the transformation of raw materials into finished products necessary in other parts of the total system. Contingency theories hold that the effectiveness of a particular organization form is *contingent* on the nature of the environmental context. Accordingly organizations must be designed by taking differences in the environment into account.

Less deterministic views recognize that organizations do have a certain amount of **control** over their environments. Advertising, for instance, helps to inform and influence customers. Large organizations sometimes command sufficient influence to affect, for instance, their markets or their legal environment. An understanding of the relationship of the organization with its environment is hence important for a rounded view of organizations.

The following section will begin by introducing some useful concepts for the analysis of environments.

ENVIRONMENT – DEFINITION

The term **environment** describes those *events, circumstances and factors* which occur *outside* the boundaries of the organization and which may influence what happens within it. This view suggests that the organization does not exist in isolation, but may be thought of as a system *existing* within a larger system (see Figure 15).

The organization system comprises those components over which its management has *direct control*. Limitation in terms of direct control is imposed by the *boundary* which separates the organization system from the environment. To some extent, management can influence what happens in the latter but does not possess direct control. The degree of reality surrounding the notion of separation depends on the permeability of the boundary. For example, to what extent does it represent a *barrier* between the organization and its environment? How easily does the organization absorb inputs from the environment and, consequently, *act* upon them in such a way as to recognize their importance? What other boundary transactions are significant?

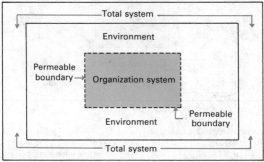

Figure 15. Systems perspective

To answer some of these questions, it is necessary to see how environments can vary. A first useful dimension is the environmental **capacity** (rich or lean); the extent to which required resources are available in the "domain" of operations of the organization. The capacity will be related to intensity of competition, creation of entry barriers, etc. A second important dimension is the **homogeneity/heterogeneity** of the environment: degree of differentiation between organizations in the environment.

While homogeneity of the environment favors development of standard procedures, heterogeneity requires either flexibility of the organization or insulation of the organization from its environment if it is too disruptive. **Stability** of the environment is a third dimension involving the degree of changes over time. Stable environments favor the older organizations that have developed fairly formalized routines. The fourth and last dimension that will be discussed is **domain consensus**: the extent to which organizations (implicitly) agree to a distribution of markets rather than competing over them, chiefly in rich environments and under oligopoly situations.

COMPOSITION OF THE ENVIRONMENT

We have referred to the environment as comprising events, circumstances and factors, and at this stage it might be helpful to determine what these are. Figure 16 illustrates some of the more important ones, identified as **sub-environments**.

Clearly, the range of influence is wide and diverse. These sub-environments will differ in their effect because each individual organization is, to some extent, operating in its own unique context, created by the particular economic and social circumstances, the nature of its trade and markets, the

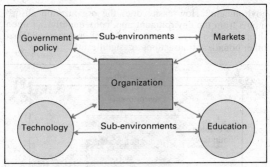

Figure 16. Sub-environments

complexity of its technology and so on. The significance of
the environment is related to the extent to which the organization is required to manage the demands which are generated. In recent years the environment has become more
complex. Consequently, the organization has had to
become increasingly analytical and sophisticated in its
approach in order to be able to handle the information
available. Organizations are likely to become increasingly
reliant on mechanisms which enable them to *scan and inter-
pret the flow of information received*. One example is the
establishment of economic intelligence units in some
businesses. Furthermore, complexity not only surrounds the
organization/environment relationship but also exists in
relationships between the environmental factors themselves. Examples are the *links* between science and technology and those relating to markets and government policy. It
is necessary for the organization to understand the nature of
such links and, more importantly, the complex forces which
can arise and affect the organization in its quest for efficiency and effectiveness.

The existence of **formal corporate planning** is an acknowledgement of such complexity, with the organization
attempting to seek a way through a maze of uncertainty. Its
survival may depend on its ability to plan well. Formaliza-
tion to this degree indicates the organization's concern with
and willingness to relate to what is happening outside its
own boundaries. It also indicates an **open systems**
approach, with the existence of control systems capable of
absorbing the requirements of change, as dictated by events,
largely out of the control of the organization.

The above approach contrasts with a **closed system** view
which is concerned with the internal functioning of the
organization and ignores the existence of phenomena outside its boundaries.

Whether it is heterogeneity, instability or domain dissensus,
organizations often need to respond in quick and adaptive
fashions; traditional highly centralized structures find difficulty in meeting this kind of reaction. Information reaching

the company from the environment may take time to digest and analyze. In a highly centralized organization there is likely to be considerable *time delay* as information is transmitted to the highest level for decisions and, when these are eventually taken, formal communication downwards through several levels of authority in the chain of command may exacerbate the problems by further delay. By the time the decision is known the information which caused it to be taken may have ceased to be of value, due to further changes within the environment. An illustration of this is where an organization becomes aware of a new market opportunity for its product but fails to react quickly enough and allows a competitor to enter the market. The process of **decentralization** which affects many companies is in part an acknowledgement of the need to locate authority and responsibility at *lower levels* in the management structure in order to speed up the rate of response to environmental change. When this is done, fewer people are involved in information flows, thus improving the time rate of decisions.

Some aspects of the environment have a more immediate effect than others, or may appear to do so to managers within the organization. Relationships with customers and suppliers are likely to be highly sensitive, and changes in these relationships will quickly become apparent, and are often directly discernible. On the other hand, economic, social and political change in the macro-environment may appear remote, particularly where such change is gradual. It may also be considerably more difficult to detect links between factors whose effects on the organization are less easy to monitor. However, such links or exchanges may be of great importance to the business. In this context research studies undertaken by Emery and Trist draw attention to the *significance of interaction* between environmental factors.

Emery and Trist (1965) attempted to produce a **typology of environmental states** which they describe in terms of a "causal" texture. They drew attention to problems created by the rate of environmental change, recognizing in particular the part played by technology, and they examined in detail **exchanges** between different parts of the environment. They emphasized that *different parts* of the environmental system may *interact* in such a way as to create conditions for the organization which are of considerable and far-reaching significance. This occurs despite the fact that such interaction is *not* directly the outcome of the organization system or of its boundary/environment transactions. Emery and Trist point to the likelihood of increasing uncertainty as an important factor.

Their identification is based on the four environmental states given below.

1. Placid randomized environment This describes an environmental state which is comparatively unchanging and where the factors – **goals and noxiants** – are distributed on a random basis. The strategy in this situation is simply that of doing.

2. Placid clustered environment This resembles the previous state in that it remains placid, but now it is possible to observe that factors relate attento each other. Organization growth occurs and **centralized** control is a feature. Strategy becomes more *distinct* and knowledge and understanding of the environment become more important.

3. Disturbed-reactive environment The outstanding feature of this type of environmental state is the presence of competitors, similar organizations in the particular market with similar objectives, each attempting to limit the other's opportunities. **Decentralized control** is often a feature of this state. Strategy now involves consideration of what others are likely to be doing.

4. Turbulent fields This characterizes an environment in which there is considerable **uncertainty** and **change** and in which environmental factors *interact* in the manner previously described. Interactions embrace both competitors and other factors and are often extremely complex and of a multiple nature.

CONTINGENCY THEORY

The contingency approach to organizations attempts to provide an explanation for the wide variety of effective organizational forms by looking at variables such as task and technology, as well as environmental factors. Burns and Stalker suggested that both mechanistic and organic types of organization could be effective depending on the stability of the market. In other words, contingency theory introduced the view that *there is no one best way to organize, though different ways are not equally effective*.

At an earlier stage we mentioned contrasting views relating to the *degree of openness* to be found between the organization and its environment, ranging from closed to open systems, with the latter providing the highest degree of interaction. Lawrence and Lorsch (1967) examined business organizations in different environments, concerning themselves with studies of important variables – notably **differentiation** and **integration** – likely to affect organization efficiency. Their examination of the organization/environment relationship was concerned with illustrating how different parts of the organization develop important relationships with different parts of the environment or, as they are more usually named, sub-environments. The latter exhibit different levels of certainty and uncertainty while the business organization can find itself experiencing both at the same time. Lawrence and Lorsch considered three dimensions in order to illustrate degrees of certainty/uncertainty.

1. Rate of change of information.
2. Time span of feedback.
3. Certainty of information.

Identification of degrees of certainty/uncertainty enables the overall classification of the environment to be either *homogeneous* or *diverse*. The existence of diversity, for example, indicates the need for structuring the organization in such a way as to enable different parts of the organization to deal with appropriate sub-environments in their own particular ways. Lawrence and Lorsch also identified a further important environmental feature, namely, the **dominant competitive issue**. For example, in the plastics industry this issue focused on new product innovation; in the container industry the issue was concerned with allocation of production facilities as related to market demand. Lawrence and Lorsch also considered the state of **interdependence between units** and found that this differed according to the particular industry. In both plastics and food industries tight interdependence was found between sales, production and research units. In the container industry tight interdependence was found between production and sales. This indicates the existence of a relationship between the dominant competitive issue in each environment *and* the pattern and degree of the interdependence between units.

Lawrence and Lorsch based their work on a study of ten firms in the container, plastics and food processing industries. Figure 17 illustrates the relationships between environmental factors and the degree of integration among organization units.

ENVIRONMENTAL FACTORS AND INTEGRATION			
Industry/firm	Type	Functional units	Need for integration
Plastics	Diverse	High differentiation	High
Food	Less diverse	Moderate differentiation	Moderate
Container	Homogeneous	Low differentiation	Low

Figure 17. Environmental factors and integration

The environment in which the plastics firm operated showed both certainty in terms of its techno-economic sub-environment and uncertainty in its production environment. The total environment was one of diversity. As a result, functional units showed considerable differentiation, demanding integration of a high order. The food firm showed less diversity and only a moderate degree of differentiation among functional units. There was *less* apparent need for integration. Studies relating to the container firm showed a homogeneous environment with low unit differentiation. The organization structure was traditional with little evidence of integration.

In sum, Lawrence and Lorsch have emphasized the dependence of the organization on market conditions and economic factors. Other theorists focused on different variables. Extensive empirical evidence has made it clear that the variance in organizational structures is not accounted for by environmental factors alone. Child (1972) identified three important variables: environment, technology, and size. There is, however, no consensus among the theorists of what factors matter for achieving the best fit between organization and environment.

MANAGING INTERDEPENDENCE

The recognition that organizations not only respond to environmental pressures but can and do modify their context, has stimulated further research. Among the earlier studies. Selznick (1949) demonstrated how organizations can mute opposition by strategies of cooptation. Selznick's study of the Tennessee Valley Authority is one of the first attempts to apply a structural analysis to the study of organizations. In order for the organization to meet its needs for stability and goal attainment, it coopted threatening outside elements by putting their representatives on the board of directors. As a consequence the representatives' loyalties were somewhat modified, at the cost however of risking to destabilize the organization itself with an eventual change in organizational objectives.

Similar strategies are widespread among organizations; they are known as **interlocking directorates**. Extensive interlocks exist between US corporations. In 1965 only 17 of the 250 largest corporations were found not to have interlocking directors with another corporation. The effects of these linkages are not clear, though Pennings (1980) argues that they will stabilize the environment by reducing market uncertainty.

A second approach in the hands of the organization is the opportunity for mergers, acquisitions or joint ventures. The extent and the duration of the assocation between two firms can vary. Between competitors such associations provide the occasion to improve the command over a market, to reduce the cost of competing, etc. Vertically interdependent organizations, i.e., supplier/customer relationships, are improved by decreasing the costs of transaction and ensuring stability in key areas of interdependence.

A final alternative, illustrating the management of interdependence, relates to purely organizational level initiatives. Hiring a competitor's executives and professionals for intelligence purposes, and price-cutting to drive out weaker competitors, are common practices. Both strategies obviously have high costs and should be considered carefully. Aggressive responses, in particular, may be less desirable than a degree of domain consensus. Indeed domain consensus can lead to mutually profitable situations. This is illustrated by the fact that informal and tacit agreements are sometimes used when explicit agreements are illegal, as in price leadership. For instance, one company takes the initiative to raise its prices with the understanding that the other companies will match the raise.

CONCLUSION

A number of important variables have been identified which were derived from a systems view of the organization and its environment. Some of the research and the conceptualizations have been presented illustrating the scope and the applicability of the theories. In the last sections less deterministic approaches were presented, showing how organizations can play active roles in shaping and choosing their own environment.

Chapter 6

Organization Politics

INTRODUCTION

Models of organization presented so far have largely neglected or even ignored the importance of organization politics. Yet inside the organization individuals and groups are found to have sometimes parochial views and private interests at odds with the organizational objectives. Furthermore, rivalries can develop which stimulate intense political activity, for instance around the acquisition of resources. Some groups or coalitions dispose of a fair amount of hierarchical power while others draw power from controlling strategic resources. This last form of unofficial power stems, for instance, from the possession of crucial technical knowledge or the control of important sources of information. It is hardly surprising under these circumstances that a good deal of political activity goes on inside the organization leading to **conflict** and changing **negotiated orders**.

Conflict describes situations in which individuals and/or groups of people are in **disagreement** with each other with the result that **inefficiencies** or **ineffectiveness** occur. The scale of inefficiency may range from minimal interference to business operations through to the occurrence of serious dysfunctions. Conflict in the organization is mostly interpersonal or structural. Interpersonal conflict can stem from the incompatibility of personalities, from competition among individuals, from divergent goals, etc. Structural forms of conflict are rooted in the interdependencies among departments and their competing or heterogeneous objectives. Organizations consist of people who, for one reason or the other, do not share the same goals or the same values. Yet organizations are mostly able to achieve a degree of internal stability. Despite the divergent interests represented in the organizational "arena," employees tend to adhere to a prevalent order with some consistency. This adherence is fundamental to the stability of collective action. Removing the assumption would lead to a rapid decay of all forms of organization. Instead it is rare that conflict grows out of hand. Contentious points come up for discussion in a relatively orderly fashion, e.g., labor contracts and budgets, to mention a few institutionalized topics of negotiation. Many other questions are less prominent but require similarly a periodic reevaluation in order to constitute acceptable practice; the legitimacy of authority, for instance, is among the questions that require periodic reassessment. In the past, management's view of the cause of conflict has been simplistic, encouraged by the perspective offered by classical organization theory and related largely to the breakdown of formal authority and the need for measures which will restore it.

If management's view is as narrow as suggested, then it is unlikely that sources of conflict other than infringement of formal authority will be identified and given genuine recognition. Any manifestation of conflict will be liable to be viewed and treated on the basis of breakdown of formal authority. Inevitably this means a lack of understanding of the many and varied sources of conflict, and suggests a situation in which management's competence to deal with conflict is limited. *Adequate understanding* and *analysis* of problems is a prerequisite of a successful treatment of conflict. If this is not forthcoming, ineffectiveness will result.

CAUSES OF CONFLICT

We can identify possible causes of conflict as follows:

1. Differences between corporate and individual goals.
2. Structural characteristics as a source of conflict.
3. Misfit between formal and informal orders.
4. Scarcity of resources.
5. Job design.
6. Individual characteristics.

Differences between corporate and individual goals

Corporate goals relate to the organization as a *total entity*. This does not mean that *each* individual in the organization will subscribe to the same goals. Each individual has his own set of goals not all of which relate to the organization, although the latter may well serve as the means whereby some at least are satisfied. *Differences* in goal identification and goal-seeking pose the possibility of conflict. A further consideration is that individuals often fulfil different roles in several organizations *simultaneously*, and where organization goals differ and/or clash this may enhance the possibility of conflict. Attitudes and commitment towards organization goals may also depend on a member's position in the hierarchy. Those who are placed at the lower end of the scale may find it difficult to identify with goals to which higher management subscribes. Perceptions of what is desirable may differ between people at different levels and these may be reinforced by notions of status and realities of organization life. In many instances, individuals may well see the organization simply as a **means of utility**, often economic, which enables the satisfaction of goals related to life outside the organization. In management's eyes individuals may not represent the desired model of **organization man** – the extent of their commitment being reflected by the views they have of the organization's role in meeting their desire for economic or social utility.

Structural characteristics as a source of conflict

Reference to a corporate goal may be suggestive of a **unitary view** at least among those who hold positions of major authority and responsibility. However, an organization consists of functions and departments built around the requirements of specialization and each unit may develop a unique view of its objectives and status within the overall framework. Different departments and groups may have quite different interests and goals. Some will be concerned

with *maintaining* the efficiency of the existing system and
their views may be primarily **inward looking**. Management
services are an example. Others will perform a more adaptive role – the marketing function, for instance, which is
primarily **outward looking**. Each will identify priorities
according to the nature of its perspective. A further form of
conflict can exist between line and staff departments. As
organizations grow and develop, they are subject to increasing specialization of function and task. As mentioned in
Chapter 3, strong staff hierarchies may develop and
encroach on what has previously been line management's
authority. A staff function may be concerned with creating a
system embodying various rules and procedures. By doing
this it is attempting to engender **conformity of action** by
those functions and departments which use its services.
However, these other functions, particularly if they are line,
may resent attempts to impose authority in this way and to
place, what some may consider, restraints on freedom of
action. They may find working within the system irksome,
particularly where the rules emanate from a function or
department to which they accord little respect and whose
actions may be seen as interference, rather than the exercise
of legitimate authority. Line personnel may seek to overrule
the system by exercising their own initiative in dealing with
problems, thus creating the possibility of inconsistencies
and increasing the likelihood of conflict. A further example
of conflict between groups is where they are *competing* for
similar roles within the organization. In practice, competition of this sort often tends to focus on certain aspects of
functional roles. For instance, the personnel function may
have overall control over staff selection policy but line
departments may also want to make actual selection decisions in relation to individual appointments. In effect, we
have a number of sub-systems and the corporate goal is the
outcome of *argument, disagreement* and *conflict* settled by
negotiation, consultation and, at times, *imposition* of authority by higher levels in the hierarchy. At times groups may be
operating under *different* frameworks of reference and this
can also lead to conflict, even where they are working with
the same information. This type of conflict may occur at the
same level within the organization. One instance is where
two or more groups of employees are competing for similar
rewards. An example is pay, where conflict cannot be viewed
as arising only out of differences between employers and
employees, but also between employees themselves who may
frequently argue and disagree over **wage differentials.**

Demarcation issues offer a further example where workers,
anxious to preserve their own security of employment, bat-
tle over what to the outsider may seem trivial differences,
but which for those involved comprise issues of considerable
magnitude, with many implications.

Misfit between formal and informal orders. The formal
organization may attempt to enforce an order that is not
necessarily compatible with the informal negotiated order.
Beliefs about technology or about how the work ought to be

done do not necessarily coincide with the official views. Furthermore, coalitions may form that pursue goals at odds with the formal goals. Formal organization may view these informal goals and beliefs as undesirable and either ignore them or actively try to suppress them. Thus conflict is generated by the tensions between the formal and the informal order.

Scarcity of resources is a major source of conflict in organizations. Groups or departments that have to compete for a resource are candidates for friction as choices have to be made about allocation. Once choices are made they can still be contested, starting another round of "politicking." Clearly the problem of scarcity is a problem of interdependence. It may be resolved by the imposition of authority (formal order), by reducing the uncertainty regarding supply, by "laissez faire" in which the contenders fight out their differences, or by eliminating the problem of scarcity altogether if additional resources can be secured by the organization.

Job design. This type of conflict may occur because of economic pressures to manufacture goods as cheaply as possible. **Economies of scale** achieved by flow line and mass production systems have meant reducing skill levels of jobs in many instances. The result may be that jobs offer little opportunity for creativity and sense of achievement and this can lead to *boredom, frustration* and *alienation* because the needs of the organization's social system are incompatible with those of the technical system. **Role conflict** can take a number of forms. One example is where the demands of the job *exceed* the capabilities of the person occupying that position. The occupant may experience role overload where he cannot cope with the physical or mental demands of the job. As a result stress may occur and produce **dysfunctional effects** which cause problems both for the organization and the individual. In this situation the job may be performed inadequately, the individual may undergo physical or psychological withdrawal and others may have to bear the burdens created by the situation.

A further example of conflict between individual **needs** and job **characteristics** is where the individual's capability exceeds the job requirement. As a result, the individual may become bored, disinterest may follow, and alienation may occur with all its associated dysfunctions. Another form of role conflict is that of **ambiguity**. This may arise either when the individual is unsure of the nature and demands of the job or where there are conflicting demands: possibly where he is responsible to different supervisors for different aspects of his role. As a result he may experience considerable *uncertainty* and stress and this may in turn give rise to conflict.

To a large extent, conflict arising from overload, underload or ambiguity has a **structural** basis although personality factors may exacerbate some of the problems. This is indicated in Figure 18.

Individual characteristics. Misadjustment among individuals may impede satisfactory working relationships. This may be due to **dissatisfaction** with real or imagined status differences, **competition for involvement** in certain areas of work, **competition for resources** or **personality clashes**. To some extent this type of conflict may serve merely as an irritant although if allowed to develop to the point where ill will becomes destructive, it may prove damaging to organization efficiency and effectiveness.

ORGANIZATION JOB FACTORS	POSSIBLE ROLE RESPONSE CAPABILITY	SITUATION	POSSIBLE OUTCOME
Demanding (physical) role	Low	Overload	Stress/conflict
Demanding (mental) role	Low	Overload	Stress/conflict
Undemanding (physical) role	High	Underload	Stress/conflict
Undemanding (mental) role	High	Underload	Stress/conflict
Ambiguous demands	Uncertainty	Overload	Stress/conflict

Figure 18. Role conflict

Conflict between individuals can also arise when they operate under **different value systems**. Some individuals prefer to see themselves as responding purely to the demands of their own set of values. They may resist pressures for conformity brought to bear on them by their colleagues. An example is where an individual refuses to join his colleagues in strike action.

REDUCING CONFLICT

Based on the identification of causes for conflict, some leads can be found as to what might defuse or reduce political activity (Pfeffer 1981). A number of such strategies must be assessed for their cost and their effectiveness.

1. Slack resources. The operation of an organization may require the existence of slack (or excess) resources. Though they involve capital and inventory costs, slack resources can simplify problems of coordination substantially by un-coupling partially different departments in the organization; slack resources decrease political activity by reducing interdependence and scarcity.

2. Group homogeneity reduces political activity by decreasing the amount of divergence regarding goals, and the means to achieve them. As a strategy, this approach involves the careful selection of entrants in terms of back-ground, education, etc., and an emphasis on training and socialization inside the organization. The cost of homogeneity strategies can be substantial, given the uniformity that it fosters; the variety of inputs is narrowed which may constitute a threat to organizations facing changing environments.

3. Deemphasizing the importance of decisions includes both the avoidance of polemical issues and deliberate underrating of important decisions. The avoidance strategy is not uncommon, though it does not appear to be sound organizational practice. In the end decisions get made *de facto* and may be of questionable quality. If the most important objective is to avoid triggering conflict, it may still be a viable alternative. Underrating important decisions, or the fractioning of important decisions in less conflict-ridden subdecisions, entails a delicate management of the steps of the decision process. These strategies can be costly in that the decisions are not debated and are likely to be made late, although quick action is necessary.

To sum up, slack resources and group homogeneity are strategies attacking the problem of conflict by modifying the premises; they are therefore relatively durable solutions. Deemphasizing the importance of decisions is, on the other hand, an attempt to change the process. This last strategy could therefore backfire if discovered, creating even more serious conflict situations.

POLITICS

Given the variety of causes for conflict, it is clear that the formal means of control, as well as the informal sources of power, will occasionally if not frequently be used to achieve a group's or an individual's ends. This situation, it should be noted, cannot be accounted for by a unitary view of the organization.

The pluralist view recognizes the existence of many different interest groups with different objectives, influenced by different value systems and working within the power structure of the organization.

Conflict resolution is seen as the outcome of a management approach which provides a system of *checks* and *balances*.

Effectively, it recognizes the legitimacy of *all* groups to pursue their claims. *Trade-off* in the form of *negotiation* ensures a degree of collaboration and may enable individuals and groups to achieve a degree of success in pursuit of their various objectives and goals.

According to the unitary view, conflict has traditionally been seen as something which is harmful and destructive to management authority and control. However, conflict viewed on the basis of the pluralist approach may be seen as a *series of interactions* between individuals and groups which enable the organization to *progress*. Indeed the alternating pursuit of goals by differing dominant coalitions results in a **variation** which is absent in rational forms of organization. Conceived as an arena, the organization is more open to innovation and change. Assuming that successful planning is limited by many imponderable factors, the trial and error process implicit in the variation process is more viable for the organization as a whole. Paradoxically, **variation** provides outcomes which enable **stability** to be achieved. The parallel to the Darwinian model of variation-selection-retention is obvious; at the population level large numbers of organizations die, while some strive and grow.

In this light conflict may be seen to serve the aims of stability and progress. Outcomes represent a basis for establishing new approaches to the question of finding solutions to problems. The existence of conflict is necessary to avoid rigidity in organizational processes. Whereas technological innovation proceeds successfully from efforts in Research and Development, organizational innovation is derived from direct implementation rather than from careful planning. As it appears that there is no one best way to organize, innovation and improvement are always possible; conflict is an important mechanism leading to new ways of doing things.

The **duality** between stability and conflict is fundamental. Conflict requires a degree of stability in order not to result in a dissolution of the organization. This measure of stability is provided by the temporary adherence to the negotiated order; never do all the mutual understandings come up for renegotiation simultaneously. On the other hand if the adopted rules never did come up for review, stability would become rigidity and the organization would not be able to respond to changing internal and external conditions. Stability can hence only be achieved on the basis of conflict.

This is adequately demonstrated in labor relations issues which are managed on the basis of consultancy and negotiation and the conduct of which is regularized to some extent by the existence of rules and procedures.

The **pluralist** approach has been criticized on the grounds that the actual basis on which negotiation takes place does *not* in fact represent a situation in which both sides have equal status. It is said that management *continues* to have authority, power and control, even when this is not invoked to its fullest extent, and that management is able to define the boundaries within which negotiation takes place and may thus limit discussion. For example, in wage discussions, debate may be concerned with the *amount* of the reward (which itself is constrained in various ways), rather than with the *basis* on which the reward is made.

Critics of the pluralist approach argue that the real substance of industrial conflict is related to the **economic** and **social fabric** of society, and that any approach which does not recognize a requirement for fundamental change is, at best, one of simple mediation.

CONFLICT MANAGEMENT

Ways of dealing with conflict vary according to its nature. Faced with the inevitability of conflict brought about by competition over resources, priorities and objectives reinforced by individual and group rivalries, organizations attempt to manage this state of affairs in such a way as to achieve at least some degree of integration.

Labor relations are controlled by the processes of industrial bargaining; this recognizes the existence of plurality of interests and of management willingness to acknowledge this state of affairs. This includes both formal and informal bargaining. However, this view may not apply to other issues where management's efforts to retain its prerogative produces at best a *benign authority*, based on ideas of human relations, but authority nevertheless. This approach focuses on the importance of *good communications* as an essential element to the clarification of situations in which conflict has occurred. Attention has also been given to the question of giving individuals greater control over what they do, based on notions of participation.

Conflict between individual and job has also been the subject of considerable attention. We have already mentioned role conflict and its consequences. An increase in division of labor and breakdown of tasks has in many instances resulted in reducing skill levels with consequent deleterious effects on social organization. The search for increasing technical and economic efficiency may have blinded organizations and managers to the *need* for a compatible social organization, so that technical and social components are viewed and treated as components of the total system. Emery and Trist (1969) have drawn attention to socio-technical systems in which change in any one component may produce change in the others. The existence of jobs with low demands in terms of skill and involvement, and possibly of interest, may offset hoped-for gains arising from technical innovation. In recent years terms such as **job enlargement** and **job enrichment** indicate attempts to reverse the trend of reducing skill levels and increasing alienation.

Chapter 7

Group Behavior

INTRODUCTION

In the course of their employment, people form individual and group relationships. Groups are a typical by-product of organizations. They arise out of the need for individuals to work together or in close proximity with one another, brought about by the demands of the work process itself or, possibly, for economic reasons, such as the use of group incentive schemes. Their existence also provides a means whereby individuals satisfy their social and psychological needs.

The importance and effects of groups and group behavior within organizations was given major prominence by the work of Mayo – the celebrated **Hawthorne experiments** – at the Western Electric Company during the period 1927–32. Earlier work by Lewin, Freud and others had drawn attention to the significance of group behavior, but the Hawthorne studies stand out as a landmark in the history of organization and management. Although the research methodology has since been the subject of critical appraisal, the studies are important in drawing attention to a more developed view of the human component in organizations, and to the significant effects of group behavior on some basis of empirical evidence. In particular, fundamental knowledge emerged about the social organization of the work group and the dynamics of behavior.

WHAT CONSTITUTES A GROUP?

A group is a collective body of people working together for their mutual benefit and in pursuit of a common goal or goals. This definition excludes collections of people who, for some extrinsic reason, are brought together momentarily – a queue for example – but who essentially remain as individuals leaving many of the characteristics mentioned above unfulfilled. Note that our definition draws attention to a number of *processes* which must occur before a group can be said to have developed its own identity.

WHAT CREATES A GROUP?

We have indicated that individuals are brought into contact with each other by the nature of their jobs. Often, work is organized in such a way as to create a group where members depend on each other for the fulfilment of their tasks. Job demands may well include the need for cooperation with other people if the job is to be discharged efficiently. For example the use of complex technology may impose a requirement for close liaison between personnel working on different aspects of a task or project. The development of social relationships, based on friendship or shared interests indirectly related to the task, may act as reinforcement to the formal requirements of cooperation.

We can distinguish two types of group:

1. Formal groups.
2. Informal groups.

Formal groups are established by the organization and are designed to accomplish the formal objectives of the business. They may arise out of the formation of departments and sections, for example, and may be based around *specialization* of function, task or job. Included within this description of formal groups are committees or teams consisting of individuals brought together for a specific purpose. An example of the latter is a project team consisting of a number of different specialists, each contributing towards the completion of the whole task. The initial reason for establishing a formal group may be reinforced when individuals are paid on a basis of group output or productivity as this may provide an incentive for the development of mutual rather than individual norms.

Informal groups develop without any formal intent of the organization, often spontaneously, on the basis of friendships, shared means and objectives or some other *common* activity. Frequently, they have *social and/or psychological* bases for their existence. In one sense their formation may be viewed as a spontaneous reaction to needs which the formal organization for one reason or another cannot fulfil. The objectives of such a group may be inconsistent with those expressed through the formal organization, and this, therefore, poses the possibility of conflict. Furthermore, they may transcend formal boundaries established within the structure, notably departmental and sectional units, and in this way gather members from all parts of the organization.

WHAT NEEDS DO GROUPS SATISFY?

These can be identified as:

1. Organization needs.
2. Individual needs.

Organization needs The obvious organization need which groups satisfy is that they provide the means whereby individuals work together so that organization objectives may be met. We have mentioned that work may demand a series of *coordinated activities* for its successful completion, with each individual within the group providing knowledge and skills. This is evident, particularly where work is organized around major tasks. *Emphasis on problem solving* creates a requirement for *cooperation, coordination* and *synergy*. The dynamics of group behavior enhance the possibility of providing effective solutions to complex tasks.

Handy (1976) refers to a range of other important functions which formal groups fulfil. Of particular note are *management* and *control, generation* of ideas and information, *test-*

ing and ratification of decisions, *coordination* of tasks, *negotiation* or conflict resolution.

Normally, groups are established for a particular purpose, but it should be noted that individuals may be members of several groups simultaneously, each of which is performing a different function from the others. Groups are an important means of achieving control over organization activity, and their use as part of the formal organization is consistent with a more **participative approach** to management whereby individuals are more fully involved in the processes of consultation and decision-making. This may enable the organization to work more effectively, recognizing the **plurality of interests** and achieving a more balanced system.

Individual needs Groups also provide a means whereby individuals satisfy a range of needs related to *social and emotional fulfilment*. The need for *affiliation*, to belong, is important for many individuals and may manifest itself in such a way as to reject behavior which carries with it the possibility of exclusion. Group membership can enable the individual to feel secure. Furthermore, it provides an opportunity for each member to establish his own identity in terms of **role fulfilment**. Individuals may view the group as providing the vehicle for the achievement of their own objective, particularly if it is one shared by others. **Mutuality of interests** may reinforce the individual's feelings of security, and it may also be felt that the group is more likely to be able to bring pressure to bear on situations, and influence decisions. Membership of the group may influence an individual member's perception of job satisfaction.

Problems may arise where formal organization and informal group needs do not coincide. At times this may place the individual in a position where he is required to exercise *choice*. He may be under considerable pressure to accede to whatever the informal group's *norm* of behavior happens to be at that point in time. This idea of a group norm suggests a *shared* belief in something which binds individuals together and to which all members are expected to subscribe, even to the point of sustaining behavior which the formal organization will reject. The individual is aware that behavior which does not support the informal group norm is likely to be frowned upon, and if the matter is considered serious to the point of undermining the group and threatening its existence, it may lead to *isolation* and ultimate *rejection* of the deviant individual. Continuing group membership is dependent on the individual's willingness to stifle his own viewpoint in favor of conforming with that of the group.

Individuals are sometimes members of several groups simultaneously and questions arise as to *how individuals manage pressure* for conformity within each group where norms between groups are incompatible. A similar situation may arise where an individual belongs to two groups, i.e. is existing physically in one, but will return to the other at some future point in time. Research undertaken by Watson and Lippitt (1955), indicates a number of possible reactions by individuals faced with this situation. Their study examined how foreign students coped with overlapping membership of groups registered both in the United States and in their home countries. They identified four main types of reaction.

1. One reaction was to identify behavior totally within the expectations of whichever group they happened to be in at the particular moment in time, and simply to ignore the existence of other groups.

2. A second reaction was where the individual identified his membership of one particular group as being more important and then behaved in ways which supported dominant group norms. This included the rejection of values arising from his other group membership which were foreign to the dominant group.

3. A third reaction was identified where the individual, when put to the test, accorded completely with the norms of one group while rejecting those of another. This behavior effectively reinforced the individual's membership of the present group but proved to be unconducive to his acceptance by the group to which he eventually returned.

4. A fourth reaction was where the individual attempted to achieve a balance between the demands created by both groups, by recognizing strengths and weaknesses in each, relating his behavior accordingly, and looking for points of contact between the strengths of each group. Here, the individual would at times be offering deviant views but in a creative way and one which it was hoped would be more likely to be acceptable to others.

This study suggests that individuals find various ways of coping with the strains and stresses of overlapping membership, attempting to *manage* the inevitable conflicts which arise. It is suggested that the fourth reaction identified by Watson and Lippitt may be indicative of a high degree of understanding of the processes of group behavior and of the problems associated with overlapping membership.

Groups are sometimes thought of as being *ineffective* in attaining their objectives. Committees, for instance, are sometimes viewed as being inefficient in their operations, wasteful of time and capable only of making poor-quality decisions. To some extent these criticisms may be justified.

FACTORS AFFECTING GROUP EFFECTIVENESS

The processes of group behavior are an important influence on the functioning of a group. Our considerations do not include discussion of whether it is appropriate for a group rather than an individual to be discharging whatever purpose is required by the organization. Our starting point is the reality that a group exists and is expected to fulfil its objectives.

First, it is apparent that individuals bring **knowledge** and **skills** to group membership. In many instances this, coupled with authority of position, is the basic justification for membership within business organizations. Knowledge and skills in this context are often thought of as relating to technical or professional expertise. For example, an engineer will be expected to contribute his own particular knowledge, as will an accountant, a management specialist, and so on. However, only to acknowledge the need for specialist skills would minimize our perception of what is important to the effective functioning of the group. The **availability** of technical knowledge and a **willingness** by individuals to make their contribution is clearly important but will only go part of the way to ensuring that the group is able to discharge its mission adequately. This could entail some modification of individual goals which each member seeks to fulfil in favor of a group goal. The mere existence and use of technical knowledge alone will not ensure that this modification happens. It may even serve to inhibit the process by helping to establish rivalries between individuals as each competes to assert his own authority in matters of technical knowledge over that of his colleagues. Thus the process of modification poses the possibility of highlighting differences, and this may lead to conflict which could make agreement even more difficult to attain.

Effective group functioning depends on the development of **supportive relationships** which, while allowing different views to be put forward and carefully considered, help the process of reaching common agreement, and **minimize the development of conflict** which could be destructive. Discussion, together with the processes of problem solving and decision-making, may well benefit from a genuinely supportive atmosphere. The individual will derive a sense of worth from being an accepted member of the group and, in turn, this may be a powerful motivating force in influencing his behavior towards other group members. This feeling of belonging to a group may go some way to meeting members' expectations in relation to their needs for support and security.

A second factor relevant for group effectiveness is the **group structure**. The pooling of knowledge and skills must be matched to the task at hand. The questions of interdependence, discussed previously, have some relevance here. Pooled, sequential, or reciprocal interdependence will obviously play a role in determining the most appropriate structure. For problem solving, centralized networks were found to be most effective if the task is elementary. When tasks are more complex, and individual inputs have to be combined, "denser" networks are more suitable; each member of the group can communicate with most of the other members.

Together, willingness to contribute and the network structure of the group substantially affect the group's effectiveness. The socio-psychological aspects that determine willingness to contribute are the most complex.

ROLE BEHAVIOR AND ITS IMPORTANCE

Certain types of role behavior can be related to:

1. Task fulfilment The exercise of skills and work undertaken in order to achieve the group's objective.

2. Group fulfilment The exercise of skills related to the social and emotional needs of the group, and the behavior of individuals in relation to such needs.

The former kind of fulfilment is concerned with the use of technical knowledge and skills possessed by each member of the group. These requisites are essentially **cognitive** in that they are employed to identify a particular problem, consider the criteria surrounding it, suggest possible alternative solutions, focus in depth on those alternatives and, eventually, arrive at a decision. Group fulfilment roles are concerned with establishing the **motivation** and **emotional security** of the group, to retain its strength and further its longevity.

Task and group skills are not to be thought of as being independent of each other. Rather they are *interdependent*. Ability to bring task skills to bear on the matter involves the use of group maintenance skills. One is seen as being *complementary* to the other.

Where both sets of skills are employed successfully, the group is more likely to be effective. The individual member has responsibility for making a contribution in both areas. His contribution will be less if he neglects or ignores the *total* requirement, or is prevented from making a full contribution by the behavior of other members.

In some ways the requirement for successful group operation parallels that of the individual manager when dealing with his department or function. His situation is not entirely similar as the *hierarchical relationship* reflecting the possibility of imposing formal authority is often more immediately apparent. His role as leader may be such that individuals defer to what they see as *legitimate higher authority*. This may serve to minimize the participation and contributions by subordinates. However, in many instances, **managerial effectiveness** may depend on the manager's ability to combine task and social skills successfully so that the needs of the task, the group and the individual are balanced to some degree. Mintzberg (1973) illustrates the varying nature of managerial work. His identification and analysis of managerial job types indicates a range of roles and processes which show some similarity to those required for successful group operation. In practice, it may be difficult to detect differences between management of some kinds of formal group, established for management purposes, and management of a department or function.

The role of **group leader** is of particular significance in the *effective* functioning of the group. The topic of leadership is dealt with in Chapter 8 but some considerations relating to groups should be reemphasized at this point.

In the first instance the leader is not the decision-maker. He is not there to force his will or views on other members in any *hierarchical*, or for that matter arbitrary, sense, although in the first instance he may take responsibility for initiating discussion and ideas. It is the *manner* or *style* in which he makes his contribution which other members may use as a yardstick in developing their perception and judgment of his leadership function. At times he may be required to allow other group members to perform functions which normally would be regarded as the leader's prerogative. In this way his role will be viewed by other members as being supportive, avoiding the destructive effects of a more hierarchical interpretation. To an extent his position will be that of first among equals. He will need to ensure that all members are making a contribution to the extent of their capabilities. Thus, he will minimize the likelihood that any individual will feel divorced or rejected from the proceedings with the possible consequences of loss of status, importance and alienation. In this way he will maximize the supportive nature of his role and enhance other members' views as to the quality of his contribution.

EFFECTIVE DECISIONS – GROUP VERSUS INDIVIDUAL

At this stage we may consider the question of whether groups are the most effective means of reaching high quality decisions.

Two points need to be made:

1. Groups are an inevitable feature of most organizations

2. Effectiveness is a function of matching task and group characteristics

Groups offer an opportunity to maximize the employment of skills which exist within the organization. However, there may be occasions when the requirement to use groups, often committees, as part of established procedure, may result in a slowing down of the decision-making process. The *benefits* of participation and involvement have to be assessed against what at times will be a need to reach decisions quickly. Where committees perform badly, the process may be a lengthy and inefficient one which may encourage feelings of frustration not only among group members but also in the minds of those who await the outcome.

The quality of decisions resides not only in the content of the decision reached but also in the extent to which participants buy into the alternative that is chosen. By developing at least a temporary commitment of group members to the decision, the implementation can be swift and smooth. Lengthy decision processes, therefore, need not be a reflection of poor group performance. A prominent example is provided by the Japanese **"ringi"** system (Ouchi 1981). A document describing the problem at hand and the solution recommended is prepared by a lower level managerial staff member. Next, the document is circulated from manager to manager in all departments that will be affected by the proposal. Each manager indicates approval by affixing his seal. Slowly the document works its way up to top management. Once the president has affixed his seal, the decision is final; the document is returned to the initiator for implementation. Though the decision process is obviously slow, implementation is usually quick since the decision has already met everybody's approval.

Studies into the question of quality of group versus individual decisions suggest that groups, on the whole, are more effective for complex tasks but can suffer certain disadvantages. Groups tend to make better decisions because of the amount of knowledge and information that is pooled and because of the variety of points of view that can be brought to bear on a particular question. Accordingly homogeneous groups (e.g., individuals with similar backgrounds) performed less effectively than heterogeneous groups (Davis 1969). Furthermore, strong group identification, under conditions of threat, tends to affect the availability of varied information and of different points of view, as well as to inhibit their expression. Janis (1972) has illustrated the problems associated with pressures towards conformity in a discussion of group decision-making under the Kennedy Administration. Wrong analysis of crucial problems seems to have resulted from a concern not to disrupt group cohesion. The dysfunctional phenomena were labeled "groupthink."

Maier (1967) examined **assets** and **liabilities** in group problem solving and concluded that the merits of group or individual approaches hinge, among other things, on the nature of the problem, quality and acceptance of the solution, and adequate communication. In particular, he focused on the importance of the *leader's role* and suggested that the success of the latter depended on how adequately the leader discharged what has been referred to earlier as group maintenance skills.

The existence of **synergy** is important to group effectiveness. Synergy describes the positive effects of pooling information and problem solving within the group. The efforts of each individual in isolation would sum up to less than the combined efforts in the group context. Basically, it arises out of the individual's willingness to release information to others and thus to offer the possibility of increasing their understanding of the problem or task under consideration. As information is given and received each participant builds upon a growing state of knowledge. This triggers better understanding, creativity and the release of additional information which would not have occurred without the *dynamics* of the interaction process. We can think of synergy as producing a level of knowledge and understanding *greater* than the sum of the individual parts, or, as it is sometimes expressed $1+1=3$. This process of synergy is vital to high levels of group effectiveness, and both task and group building skills contribute to its outcome. (See Figure 19.)

SUMMARY

The discussion of group behavior has pointed to the presence of two kinds of groups in the organization: formal and informal groups. Informal groups are probably most difficult to control. However, even formal groups present substantial difficulties to the manager. Problems of effectiveness stem both from the difficulty of finding an appropriate fit between task and group structure and from cognitive processes taking place within the group. Altogether, groups appear to be potentially very effective, though this effectiveness rests on fragile equilibria that are mostly beyond the immediate control of management.

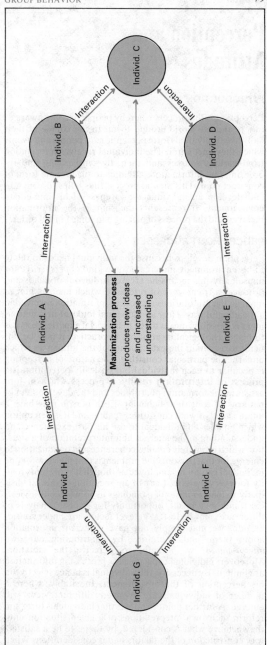

Figure 19. Synergy process

Chapter 8

Perception and Attitudes

INTRODUCTION

Perception is the process whereby people become aware of others and the world around them. In the course of their daily lives individuals form perceptions of people and events which they encounter. The individual receives information from various sources and then, by synthesizing and re-ordering that information, attempts to place some form of construct on it. This mental process thus helps to structure and develop an individual's awareness of his immediate environment. It represents the sum of the information received and the process of placing it in some kind of order.

PERCEPTION PROCESSES

Perception develops because the individual needs to relate to his environment and create some kind of *perspective* for himself. By this means he creates order out of chaos and produces a framework of reference which enables him to manage the multifarious sources of information received in a meaningful way. How an individual looks at his environment is, possibly, due as much to his social experience as it is to his psychological disposition. In practice, it may be difficult to ascertain the exact nature of the influences which underlie the particular construct. The nature of perception is peculiar to each individual but basically perception is a process of **interpreting reality**, a process which in turn assists in the formation of attitudes and the development of patterns of consistent behavior. Each person may have a unique view of what constitutes reality, and it is perception which enables an individual to use his past experience and understanding in the analysis and interpretation of a situation which ultimately enables coherence and organization to emerge for that person. One problem is that the view for one individual cannot be employed as though it represents reality for everyone else. Lack of appreciation of this factor is likely to lead to misunderstandings as to why contra views exist and, as a result, opportunity for realistic analysis of differences may be lost. Whatever factors are under consideration, we may simply not have sufficient information about them, and, therefore, by contributing our own *interpretation*, we attempt to perceive the situation. Moreover, individual capacities for processing information are limited. By necessity, the individual is hence selective in his perception of the environment. Inevitably, where a number of individuals are involved, different views will emerge. A further point to note is that individuals form and reform their own intepretations of a given situation until they achieve what is considered, by them, to be a satisfactory construction of the factors under consideration. When an individual indicates a lack of understanding of another person's point of view, it may be that the individual is applying his own perceptions and points of reference to an explanation of that other person's behavior. This can make effective communication difficult, and processes of understanding, consultation and negotiation may be inhibited. Frequently, *emotions* may be involved and serve as a means of reinforcement to the process of developing perceptions. A sense of *security* is involved in the achievement of a satisfactory framework of reference and, therefore, the individual may be reluctant to abandon particular attitudes and behavior which enhance his security. To this extent, the individual may be *selective* in relation to his use of information, facts and circumstances. He may tend towards selecting those factors which support his existing perceptions. By this means he retains his sense of security and is likely to *reject* or *distort* information which is incompatible with his views. This process may be viewed as acting at the level of the subconscious and should not necessarily be construed as pertaining to deliberate distortion. The individual seeks information which fits in with what his picture of reality already suggests is appropriate.

A further problem which may arise concerns the existence of **distortion**. The individual is faced by numerous events and circumstances many of which cannot be ignored altogether. We have described the process of selectivity as affording one way in which the individual copes with his *milieu*. However, this particular process is only one of many and cannot adequately describe all circumstances. Not all information reaching the individual can be rejected, and in this circumstance a new way of coping with the threat to security may emerge – a process which involves distortion. Here, information is reorganized in such a way that it will fit the perceptual framework of the individual. The information has meaning only when related to the individual's particular view of the circumstances under consideration. Any item of information received which does not fit the pattern required may be reinterpreted in such a way as to make it fit. This process of modification, involving distortion, occurs subconsciously for much of the time and, as with selectivity, enables the individual to retain his feelings of order and security. Figure 20 illustrates the perception process.

The above description of individual processes of perception must be completed with a short summary of the interpersonal processes. In the first chapters of this book the importance of shared understandings was described in the context of social action theory. If one individual is attempting to communicate a message to another, he will be successful to the extent that his message relies on a set of notions, the meaning of which is shared. Simple, concrete messages will almost certainly get across as they rely on widely-shared, common concepts. But the more abstract or complex the relevant concepts, the more a successful communication will require a unique body of shared meanings. This does not preclude the fact that each individual may have a unique view of reality. But in communicating, each person has to "put himself in the other person's shoes" to achieve a construct of information similar to the one being undertaken by that person. In practice this is very difficult to achieve. It makes great demands on the individual in terms of his sensitivity to the needs of the other person and, in consciously striving to understand a viewpoint other than his own, he may have to abandon his own strongly held and cherished ideas. However, if the attempt is not made, then adequate communication becomes much harder to achieve, and this may have some influence on creating and sustaining effective relationships.

THEORIES OF PERCEPTION

The question arises as to how the process of perception works. One approach is to view it as being **intuitive**. For example, is the judgment immediate, following assimilation of facts and circumstances?

Theories concerned with intuition involve considerations of whether perception occurs **directly**, whether it is **innate** and whether it is **total** – that is, the individual identified or understood in terms of his **whole** personality. One popular theory within the intuitive school is **Gestalt theory**. Fundamentally, this view propounds the notion that the whole is greater than the sum of its individual parts, and that the brain organizes or adds information to the other information inputs it receives. It relates to perception in that, for example, one individual in communication with another *conveys* to that person some knowledge of his *psychic disposition*. The information is conveyed through some *physical* expression such as a facial movement. The other person in the relationship sees this, and through his own psychic processes can perceive and understand that individual. This is known as **isomorphism**.

Another view relates to the development of **empathy** between individuals in communication with each other. This theory states that one person understands how the other feels because he is able to visualize himself in a similar situation.

A second school of theory in relation to perception is concerned with the process of **inference**. This view considers that the individual creates his framework of reference by a process of inference accrued from the knowledge available. For example, a proposition based on inference would work as follows.

1. Individuals with firm handshakes have strong characters.
2. This individual has a firm handshake.
3. This same individual is of strong character.

What has happened is that statement 3 is inferred from our perceptions surrounding statements 1 and 2. Our **reasoning process** has concluded that statement 3 is correct

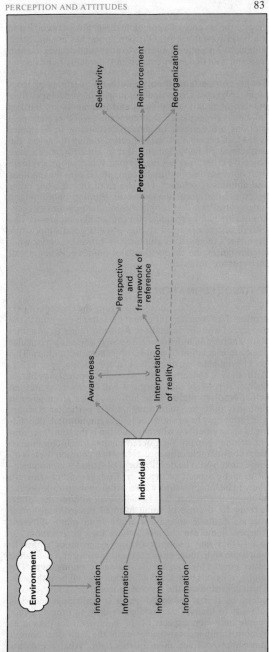

Figure 20. Perception processes

despite the absence of a complete direct link between it and
the first two statements. Our perception has assumed that
statement 3 is a reasonable one to adopt and derives its truth
from our *scan* and *interpretation* of statements 1 and 2.

Social comparison theory addresses questions of judgment criteria, as opposed to judgment processes. In a
number of situations opinions and judgments are hard to
validate, yet people need to determine whether their perceptions are correct. In general, according to Festinger
(1954), a person will use objective reality to assess the
correctness of his judgment. But in circumstances where
objective criteria are not readily available, "people evaluate
their opinions and abilities by comparison with the opinions
and abilities of others." The choice of the relevant other
becomes, therefore, important in forming opinions and
judgments. Peers and people with similar opinions or background are likely candidates for the social comparison. The
overall results of recent studies provide good support for
Festinger's theory. It is still unclear, however, under what
circumstances the theory does not hold, i.e., when social
referents are not used.

ATTITUDE FORMATION

We have discussed notions surrounding the concept of perception. To a considerable extent the latter is essential to the
process of attitude formation. **Attitude** refers to a mental
state whereby an individual is *disposed* towards a particular
response in relation to people, objects and situations. This
goes beyond how we might, for example, define personality.
Attitudes are concerned with what an individual may like or
dislike. It is likely that emotions will be involved and the
actual **emotive state** of the individual at a given point in
time may influence the formation of a particular attitude.
The latter may be of short- or long-term duration, depending to some extent on whether emotion is the sole determinant or one of many such determinants which continue to
exert considerable influence even when emotion itself is no
longer involved. The development of attitudes is *fundamental* to many aspects of behavior. Changes in behavior are
likely to be longer lasting where a change in attitude occurs,
although the former can be achieved without the latter,
perhaps by the use of some form of reward/punishment
system. Attitude formation arises from many different
sources. Some are *cultural*, others may be *economic* or
social – they may be derived from the group or groups in
which the individual circulates and may form a *consistent*
pattern with a high degree of *consonance* among them. The
family, religious belief and education may all be influences
which contribute to the state of consonance. A further consideration is that the **logic** which an individual adopts is
relevant to himself, but not necessarily to others. Other
people may view aspects of the behavior of a person as
demonstrating inconsistencies while the individual himself
may simply not see them in this light. What represents
rationality to one person may be seen as irrational by others.

This suggests that knowledge in itself may be insufficient as a basis for attitude formation. It is the way in which the knowledge is used – the **rationalization process** used to defend a particular view – which is also an important factor in attitude development.

The history of research into attitudes, and particularly attitude change, is a long and detailed one. In the field of social psychology, attitude research has been viewed as being of prime importance. In particular, Allport (1935) drew attention to its importance in enabling the development of social psychology as a definitive area of study. In a volume of this size it is impossible to adequately examine the total nature of theoretical studies in attitude change. However, when discussing perception, mention was made of the nature of Gestalt psychology with its essentially **cognitive** approach. In more recent times considerable attention has been given to the development of **balance theories**. Fundamentally, these are based on the premise that the individual attempts to *achieve consistency* among his various attitudes and that psychological pressures exist to arrange new information received in such a way that it fits with his existing attitudes. In particular, Festinger (1957) postulated a theory of **cognitive dissonance**. He examined various cognitive inputs received by the individual recognizing that certain of these may be **consonant** to each other, that is they are in agreement or have some basis of commonality, while others may be **dissonant**, i.e. out of agreement. It is the latter state which creates problems because associated with this condition is a degree of psychological unhappiness. For example, an individual may perceive trade unions as being undesirable and form unfavorable attitudes towards them. However, he may work within an environment where unionism is strongly supported. His cognitions in respect of this situation are dissonant, i.e. they are at odds with each other and are out of balance, and he will experience pressures to restore them to a state of balance. People desire cognitions which are consonant and therefore seek to find ways of achieving or re-achieving this state. In the example quoted, possibilities open to the individual include a situation where the individual *disassociates* himself from his work colleagues to such an extent that their views are no longer of significance – here the discordant aspect is being removed – or the individual changes his mind about unions so that they are then similar to those of his colleagues. His perceptions are then in a state of balance and psychological happiness is restored.

Much will depend on the *degree of importance* which the individual attaches to the particular issues and the extent to which he experiences unhappiness. The *centrality* of the attitude, that is, its importance to the individual, will have a considerable influence on whether that individual is willing to change his viewpoint and behavior. If the level of importance is high, then dissonance may be tolerated despite the problems it brings.

Associated with the notion of attitude change is a concept which attempts to provide further explanation of the process. This is known as **reinforcement theory** and is based on the proposition that if an individual behaves in a certain way, and such behavior is rewarded, then he is more likely to behave in a similar way in the future. The usefulness of this consideration will depend to a large extent on the *value* that the particular individual places on the potential reward. However, it does present the possibility that an organization, through its management, can use the rewards at its disposal to influence the behavior of subordinates. Of course, in practice, organizations do use rewards to commend behavior which is regarded as appropriate. However, the nature of the influence involves a process of shaping the individual's responses in such a way that he will learn to *cooperate*, and carries with it anticipation that over a period of time such *conditioning* will result in the development of attitudes favorable to the organization's objectives.

ATTITUDES AND COMMUNICATION

The whole question of perception and attitude formation has considerable implications for communication as a **control process** within the organization. In terms of two people communicating with each other in a manager/subordinate relationship, *each person* in the transaction has something to gain from a situation where communication is effective. For the manager it enables the possibility of increasing the subordinate's understanding of the organization's objectives. For the subordinate, effective communication provides an opportunity to create a picture for himself of how he contributes to the organization's objectives, and how his role fits into the broader perspective of the total organization. Both parties can gain from improved understanding which itself must be influenced to a considerable degree by the processes of attitude formation, including the extent to which the constitution of reality is shared. However, it requires more than each party hearing what the other has to say. There has to be some degree of understanding which relates to the other person and some acceptance of what that understanding implies. This may involve a proposed course of action being modified to take account of what the other person requires.

SUMMARY

Perception and attitudes are closely related to motivation which is the subject of the next chapter. To consider motivation in isolation, devoid of considerations of perception and attitudes, would be to neglect provision of an adequate base for consideration of the topic.

Chapter 9

Motivation at Work

INTRODUCTION

Continuing on the theme of individual behavior in organizations, one area of fundamental importance to managers is why different individuals doing the same job perform at different levels. Differences in performance can be attributed to two factors. Firstly, individuals will have varying abilities according to their education, training and experience. Therefore, in attempting to maximize performance, managers should ensure that their work force have suitable abilities to perform in a job successfully. They can endeavor to do this through recruitment and selection procedures, the design of training programs or, if necessary, by altering the job content to ensure it matches the ability of the employee. Secondly, differences in performance levels may be due to different levels of individual motivation. Individuals vary in their willingness to direct their efforts towards the achievement of organization goals. Thus:

Performance = function (**ability** level × **motivation**)

This chapter concentrates on the topic of motivation. If managers are to take decisions to improve the performance of individuals so that they may make a greater contribution to organization effectiveness, the managers will require an understanding of motivation. The principles behind motivation form the basis for numerous managerial decisions; for example, the design of jobs, the design of wage and salary systems and the style of leadership to be adopted.

Motives are the forces underlying human behavior, and the stimulus for action is the desire to satisfy personal needs or wants. **Motivation** is the willingness to exert effort in order to achieve a desired outcome or goal which will satisfy someone's needs. The basic model of motivation is thus:

Need $\longrightarrow$ Action $\longrightarrow$ Goal

e.g. thirst for $\longrightarrow$ drinking water $\longrightarrow$ quenching of
water thirst

Action is thought to cease if the goal fulfils the need; any gap between the goal and the need will lead to further action.

In the context of work the individual must satisfy his own needs through job performance while at the same time meeting organization criteria of effectiveness. Simple as this may sound the subject of work motivation has attracted considerable research and, as with many areas of human relations, its complexity limits the extent of our understanding. It is not easy to make predictions about which needs will give rise to a particular form of behavior which in turn may be directed towards achieving organization goals. Moreover, needs vary between individuals, and each individual's needs may vary over time. Theories which have been developed can be divided into two categories:

1. Content theories which address the question of what motivates people. These seek to identify the needs which cause individuals to perform in certain ways.

2. Process theories which address the question of how certain actions are determined. These concentrate on the thought processes which individuals undergo before being motivated to act in a certain way.

CONTENT THEORIES

Four content theories will be examined:

Maslow's Hierarchy of Needs.
McClelland's Achievement Motivation.
McGregor's Views of Man.
Herzberg's Two Factor Theory.

Maslow's Hierarchy of Needs

Maslow, an American psychologist, was one of the first major researchers to differentiate between needs, and draw a distinction between higher and lower order needs. Maslow's hypotheses on the nature of motivation (1954) comprise a hierarchy of five levels of needs which, arranged in ascending order of relative importance to the individual, are as follows.

1. Physiological The essentials for survival such as the desire for food, water, air and sleep.

2. Safety The desire for security and protection against danger.

3. Social The desire to fulfil the need for belonging, for love and affection.

4. Esteem Exhibited in two ways: firstly, self-esteem, which is the need for self-respect, and secondly, esteem from others, which is the need for respect from others – the need for recognition.

5. Self-actualization More difficult to define but viewed as the need for self-fulfilment, of striving to realize one's full potential.

In Maslow's hierarchy of needs, illustrated in Figure 21, (1)–(3) are considered lower order needs while (4) and (5) are considered higher order needs.

Individuals can pass to higher order need levels only when the lower order needs are satisfied. Thus, physiological needs must be satisfied to some acceptable level before an individual will pass upwards to pursue safety needs and so on up the hierarchy until self-actualization is reached. Once a need is satisfied it no longer monopolizes an individual's behavior; behavior will be directed towards satisfying the next need level. The corollary is obvious – only unsatisfied needs act as motivators. However, the exception to this is self-actualization where increased satisfaction, instead of decreasing need strength, tends to increase the desire for further self-fulfilment. Complete satisfaction of self-actualization is rarely, if ever, achieved.

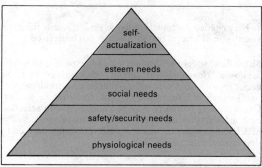

Figure 21. Maslow's hierarchy of needs

Maslow's theory presents needs conceptually and to define them in operational terms which can be empirically tested is problematic. He did not design the theory specifically for the organization setting, rather it applied to the total life situation of the individual. Clearly, needs may be satisfied outside work and questions can be raised as to the applica-bility of the theory to industry, though, as seen later, subse-quent writers have applied the self-actualizing approach to the industrial setting. Maslow highlighted the importance of **intrinsic motivation:** this is motivation stemming from within the individual, which raises questions on how work might be structured to facilitate individual satisfaction of higher order needs. Conversely, **extrinsic motivation** results from factors external to the individual, for example, pay.

The intuitive appeal of the hierarchical model has made it extremely popular among managers; the hypotheses lack, however, empirical support. Only the distinction between higher and lower order needs has shown some degree of empirical validity.

McClelland's Achievement Motivation
Implicit in Maslow's higher order needs is the desire for achievement or accomplishment. Using personality tests, McClelland (1961) studied the characteristics of people whom he identified as being **achievement orientated**. High-need achievers were always exhibiting behavior designed to better themselves, working harder in order to accomplish their goals. They shared a number of common characteristics:

1. Preference for performing tasks over which they had sole responsibility, to enable them to identify closely with the successful outcomes of their actions.

2. They were moderate risk takers, and to maximize their chances of success they set themselves moderate goals. This does not mean to say that they avoided challenging situations, but simply that their goals were within an attainable range.

3. They needed continual feedback, since it is only from the knowledge of success that satisfaction can be derived.

McClelland sought to discover why some people were low achievers. He concluded, among other things, that the major reasons lie in parental influences, education, cultural background and the value systems dominant in society. Organizations therefore may be concerned with selecting high achievers as managers but, even more significantly, McClelland suggested that low achievers can be trained to develop a greater urge to achieve.

McGregor's View of Man

McGregor attempted to apply some of Maslow's thinking to the work context. He argued that managers' decisions to influence individual behavior at work were based on their assumptions about human nature. Some of these assumptions have already been touched upon in the examination of approaches to the study of organizations (Chapter 1). McGregor divided managerial assumptions about human nature into two schools of thought, **Theory X** and **Theory Y**. He suggests that a Theory Y view is more appropriate to the pursuit of organization effectiveness than a Theory X view.

Taylor's scientific management is associated with the **economic man** view of human nature and McGregor's Theory X provides a complete picture of the assumptions behind this view. The notion of economic man is rooted in the idea that individuals at work are motivated to direct their actions towards organization objectives by the promise of financial rewards. Money is the major motivator and therefore individual performance can be controlled by incentive payment schemes since workers will automatically increase their productivity in return for money. The Theory X view of human nature incorporates the following assumptions:

1. The average person inherently dislikes work and whenever possible will avoid it.

2. As a result of assumption 1 people must be coerced, controlled, directed and threatened with punishment to direct their effort towards achieving organization goals.

3. Most people at work want to avoid responsibility, have little ambition and are mainly concerned with lower order needs.

Accordingly work was sub-divided into numerous tasks which were often of a repetitive nature and were controlled by predetermined methods of working that provided little opportunity for discretion.

While the remaining theories in this chapter criticize the economic approach it would be wrong to underestimate the importance of pay to individuals. Despite criticisms of the operations of payment by results schemes and the Theory X view, payment by results schemes are still fairly widely used in certain industries, e.g. manufacturing. **Payment by results** schemes are when management agrees to pay an employee an agreed sum of money for his output level. Since workers are paid according to the units or pieces of output they produce, this system is sometimes referred to as piecework. Where there is a direct relationship between pay and the amount produced this is viewed as straight piecework though the incentive element, i.e. the ratio of pay to output level, may vary according to the type of scheme operated.

Among researchers concerned with the motivation of individuals it was the *restriction of output* under incentive pay schemes which raised doubts about the validity of the economic man approach. Workers tended to restrict output in the fear that if they performed too well management might change the rate. Obviously workers prefer a loose rate, i.e. one which allows them to earn bonuses relatively easily, and so they develop practices to avoid a tighter rate being introduced by management. Workers restrict output in line with group norms and therefore set their own output standards. The motive may be the protection of slower workers or fears for job security. Alternatively, workers may decide to peform at levels of output which offer them a stable earnings profile.

It was evident that payment by results schemes could be a "two-edged sword" for management, though acting as a managerial control technique it provided work groups with a substantial degree of control over their own effort levels. The importance of social relations in work groups and the establishment of group norms of behavior prompted a reaction to the emphasis on economic man. **The Human Relations School** developed an alternative view of man, labelled the **social man view**. As mentioned in Chapter 1, this view emphasized the social factors at work; for example, the significance of the informal organization, managerial leadership styles and effective communication systems.

While, in some companies, the benefits of operating a payment by results scheme outweigh the costs, industrial relations pressures may prompt some large companies to switch to an alternative system. Time rate systems which link earnings to hours of attendance rather than directly to actual performance levels may be considered less desirable for production workers since there is little incentive to work harder. Measured day work became a popular alternative in some circles since it combined elements of both time rate and payment by results. In this system employees are paid an agreed level of earnings in return for a specified level of performance. Many companies in the automobile industry have changed to this method of payment.

However, it is not the intention of this book to discuss payment systems in detail though it should be obvious that the selection of any particular system will depend on a number of variables, especially the technology used in the production process.

To reiterate, most organizations realize the significance of pay as an incentive to improve performance, and to criticize the economic approach does not mean that pay is not important to individuals as has been verified in a number of studies (a point returned to later in this chapter). However, management must realize that the importance attached to pay may vary between individuals and that they have other needs to fulfil as well as economic needs. For this reason the rational economic man approach must give way to other assumptions about human behavior in organizations.

McGregor has taken the social man view a stage further with his Theory Y. In parallel with Maslow's theory and later Herzberg's theory, Theory Y depicts man's motives as being more than simply the desire for money or social contact. Instead man is seeking self-fulfilment and self-actualization and it is not surprising that this view, associated with the **Neo-Human Relations School**, has been called the **self-actualizing man approach**. The managerial assumptions comprising McGregor's Theory Y, which are in essence Maslow's concepts tailored to the organization setting, are as follows:

1. The average person does not dislike work for work can be a source of satisfaction.
2. People can exercise self-direction and self-control at work.
3. People may seek to satisfy higher order needs as well as lower order needs at work.
4. People are keen to accept responsibility at work and may be capable of creativity.
5. In modern industrial life the average person is not being utilized to his full potential.

The Theory Y view has obvious implications for the managerial leadership styles discussed in Chapter 10. It also highlights the importance of intrinsic motivation, emphasizing the higher order needs of individuals which they seek to satisfy through their jobs. The corollary is that if management creates the work environment in which individuals can realize their higher order needs, then they will perform more effectively and efficiently in the pursuit of organization objectives and as a result will be more satisfied in the process.

McGregor also makes the interesting point that whatever

the assumptions management adopt, they can represent a self-fulfilling prophecy. For example, if you manage according to the assumption that people are basically lazy and uninterested in work *per se*, then it is likely that employee behavior will reflect this assumption.

The final content theory within the self-actualizing man approach is Herzberg's two factor theory which is still very influential in current managerial thinking.

Herzberg's Two Factor Theory (Motivation-Hygiene Theory)

Unlike Maslow, Herzberg's theory was specifically designed to improve our understanding of people at work, in particular the factors which determine **job satisfaction** and **job dissatisfaction**. His conclusions were based on a research survey covering some 200 accountants and engineers who were asked to recall the reasons for feeling exceptionally good and/or bad at certain times in their work. He discovered, after analyzing the causes for satisfaction and dissatisfaction, that these two variables were not opposites but two distinct, independent dimensions. The findings are summarized in Figure 22.

The equations indicate the independent nature of the two variables. The removal of dissatisfaction by adjusting the hygiene factors will not cause satisfaction, which can be achieved only by taking account of the motivator factors. The determinants of job satisfaction are the intrinsic aspects of the job which emanate from the content of the job and satisfy higher order needs. The determinants of job dissatisfaction are the extrinsic aspects of the job which relate to the context of the job and satisfy lower order needs.

What are the implications of Herzberg for management decision-making which seeks to influence individual job performance? Like McGregor, Herzberg is suggesting that managers must move away from their traditional concentration upon the extrinsic factors and redesign jobs so that the individual has greater scope for autonomy, responsibility and the opportunity for personal growth. The redesign of jobs in this way is known as **job enrichment**, previously mentioned in Chapter 3.

In the literature, job enrichment is sometimes referred to as **vertical job enlargement**. Job enrichment is one of four methods of job redesign which has been applied in a number of companies. The other methods are as follows:

1. Job rotation This involves moving workers between a number of jobs on some regular time basis so as to introduce some variety into the activities performed by the employee.

2. Job enlargement (sometimes referred to as horizontal job enlargement). This involves changing the content of a specific job in order to build in additional tasks which do not require any increase in responsibility levels.

3. Autonomous work groups Experiments in autonomous work groups are closely related to the socio-technical systems approach which attempts to derive the optimal match between technological requirements, social needs and economic factors. (See the coal-mining study mentioned in Chapter 1.) These experiments involve groups of workers engaged in a complete area or unit of work, e.g. assembling engines, dispatching goods, who are given considerable autonomy and control over how they perform the unit of work. This often enables the group to be responsible for its own planning, organization and coordination of tasks.

Herzberg's theory was directly applied in a series of job enrichment experiments carried out by Imperial Chemical Industries (ICI) in the late 1960s and reported by Paul and Robertson in their book *Job Enrichment and Employee Motivation* (1970). The experiments covered a variety of occupational groups – sales representatives, design engineers, experimental officers, draftsmen, production and engineering foremen and blue collar workers. The jobs in a selected experimental group were enriched and the results were compared to that of a control group whose jobs had not been changed in any way.

Summarizing the experiment with the production and engineering foremen, a number of job changes were introduced. Examples of these changes were as follows: production foremen were given the authority to alter loading and sequencing schedules, to select their own employees and to take decisions on non-standard payments; engineering foremen were given greater control over preventative maintenance work and some budgetary control; and all foremen were assigned special projects, given greater disciplinary powers (short of dismissal), granted responsibility for the assessment, training and development of their subordinates and were generally accorded greater recognition for reaching their targets.

Comparing some results of the performance of the experimental groups with those of the control groups, the former appeared markedly better; the number of disputes engaged in were reduced and were settled more quickly; recruits selected by production foremen were considered to be of a better quality than those previously selected and job satisfaction was generally higher.

Experiments with the white collar groups all showed some degree of success though experiments with blue collar workers (tool setters and process operators) were less successful in this particular case.

Most of the results of experiments were measured in terms of the quality of production, labor turnover, absenteeism and overall job satisfaction, all of which were normally positive. Interestingly, job enrichment has not always led to increased productivity.

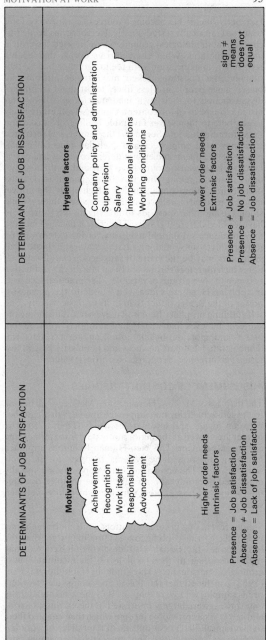

DETERMINANTS OF JOB DISSATISFACTION

sign ≠ means does not equal

Hygiene factors

Company policy and administration
Supervision
Salary
Interpersonal relations
Working conditions

Lower order needs
Extrinsic factors

Presence = Job satisfaction
Presence = No job dissatisfaction
Absence = Job dissatisfaction

DETERMINANTS OF JOB SATISFACTION

Motivators

Achievement
Recognition
Work itself
Responsibility
Advancement

Higher order needs
Intrinsic factors

Presence = Job satisfaction
Absence ≠ Job dissatisfaction
Absence = Lack of job satisfaction

Figure 22. Herzberg's two factor theory

Herzberg's theory has become a source of controversy, for it could be empirically tested. Firstly, Herzberg has been criticized on methodological grounds where he used the critical incident method. What characterizes events that people remember, in association with feeling good or bad? Additionally, the questions asked may trigger attributional biases, since people are less likely to attribute feelings of dissatisfaction to their own inadequacies and may refer instead to aspects of job content. Conversely, they are likely to attribute to themselves favorable feelings of satisfaction in performing the job. Secondly, the sample was restricted to professional employees and excluded blue collar employees. Subsequent studies in different countries and covering a range of work groups have provided conflicting evidence, some agreeing with Herzberg's conclusions, some disagreeing. Interestingly, studies which apply the critical incident method usually confirm Herzberg's theory while studies using other methods to investigate job satisfaction have yielded different results. The critical incident method may introduce substantial biases by relying extensively on retrospective sense-making. Later studies indicate that *motivators* may be the cause of satisfaction *and* dissatisfaction which therefore throws doubt on Herzberg's distinction between the two groups of variables. The practical successes in applying Herzberg's ideas can be due to the persuasive power of the theory rather than to its intrinsic validity. The self-fulfilling prophecy here is that everybody, including the subjects, believes that variety and autonomy will lead to a better and more enjoyable job. Long-term results will demonstrate what part newness and popularity play in fostering performance, as opposed to intrinsic value.

ASSESSMENT OF CONTENT THEORIES

The theories of Maslow, Herzberg and McGregor all belong to the self-actualizing man approach and each distinguishes between higher and lower order needs (Figure 23). The former are viewed as the major motivating force influencing employee behavior. This Neo-Human Relations approach has been questioned by systems theorists for its oversimplification. The conclusion that people are intrinsically motivated does not take account of the complex dynamic interaction of a host of other variables which differ between situations.

Studies reveal that in some situations some individuals may weight the extrinsic job factors as more important than the intrinsic ones. Individuals' attitudes to their job content may differ according to their skill level, their cultural background or personality. The study by Goldthorpe *et al.* (1968) concluded that the skilled and semi-skilled workers of his sample, who were employed in three manufacturing enterprises, were largely interested in the extrinsic factors, and saw work as providing income which then enabled them to meet unfulfilled needs outside of their place of work (*an instrumental orientation*). This study and other similar ones have not been without criticisms. Management could inter-

Theorist	Higher order needs	Lower order needs
Maslow	Self-actualization Esteem	Social Safety/security Physiological

Herzberg	Motivator factors:
	  Achievement
	  Recognition
	  Work itself
	  Responsibility
	  Advancement
		Hygiene factors:
		  Company policy
		  and administration
		  Supervision
		  Salary
		  Interpersonal
		  relations
		  Working conditions

McGregor	Theory Y view of man	Theory X view of man

Figure 23. Similarities between content theories

pret these studies as saying that if workers are interested in extrinsic factors (especially pay and job security) then there is no reason to consider how their jobs might be altered to provide the opportunity to fulfil higher order needs. The problem is that people who are claimed to value the extrinsic aspects are often employed in jobs of little intrinsic worth and perhaps if they had the opportunity to work in more intrinsically rewarding jobs their attitudes might change.

The debate continues and in reality it is probably safe to assume that people are generally concerned with both the intrinsic and extrinsic rewards; for example managers may find it difficult to redesign jobs to improve intrinsic worth if employees are worried about pay or job security being endangered. However, the discussion does throw doubts on the over-simplified and generalized conception of man presented in the self-actualizing man approach. This has been met with an alternative view of individual behavior, **the complex man approach**, devised by Schein (1965). In terms of organization theory this approach is closely allied to systems theory. The five underlying assumptions of the complex man approach are as follows:

1. Man's motives are complex and may change over time or with the circumstances of the situation in which he finds himself.

2. Man can learn new motives from his experience.

3. Man's motives may differ according to the organization or job.

4. The link between job satisfaction and productivity is not as direct as previously implied by the self-actualizing approach (further developed in the next section).

5. Man will respond to different managerial strategies to improve his performance and there is no single strategy which will succeed for all workers at all times.

The process theories of Vroom and Porter and Lawler take account of many of these assumptions.

PROCESS THEORIES

As indicated at the beginning of this chapter, process theories concentrate not on what motivates people at work but how they are motivated. This is done by examining the process which individuals go through before behaving in a certain way. Individual differences may occur because people's expectations vary and the theories are sometimes referred to as **expectancy theories**. Expectancy theory is a **cognitive theory** of motivation since it assumes individuals are consciously aware of goals and direct behavior rationally towards attaining those goals. **Non-cognitive theories** are sometimes referred to as **stimulus-response theories** in that behavior is caused by external stimuli and hence the internal processes occurring within the individual are largely ignored. The origin of expectancy theory can be traced back to the writings of Tolman in the 1930s but one of its earliest applications for motivation at work was via what has been termed a "path-goal approach." **Path-Goal Theory** implies that the individual can choose which goals he wishes to pursue and the paths which will direct him towards their attainment. The theory was originally formulated by Georgopoulous, Mahoney and Jones (1957) who sought to explain why individuals were motivated to produce at different levels. They argued that the motivation to produce at a certain level was due to the particular needs of an individual which will be expressed in goal-directed behavior. So if productivity is perceived as a path to attaining these goals then the individual will produce at a higher level provided that pathway is free from blockages.

Vroom's Expectancy Theory (1964) of motivation is considered one of the first major formulations of expectancy theory. Vroom explains motivation as being a function of three factors:

1. Valence (V) This is the preference an individual has for a particular outcome. It is the individual's perception of the satisfaction he will gain if he achieves the particular outcome.

2. Expectancy (E) This is a subjective probability measure that doing something will actually lead to a particular outcome.

3. Force (F) This is another term for motivation resulting from the interaction of valence for various possible outcomes and the expectancy that action will lead to those outcomes.

The relationship between these factors is given in the following equation:

MOTIVATION $F = f \Sigma (E \times V)$

where $V =$ expectancy that action will be followed by a desired outcome
$E =$ strength of preference for a particular outcome
$\Sigma =$ summation sign, included since a particular course of action typically has more than one outcome.

Individuals then, are motivated to behave in certain ways by choosing from a range of possible outcomes the ones which have the best odds of occurring.

At work, where employees have high expectations of a desired outcome occurring, they will exert considerable effort in their job towards achieving that outcome. For example, if an individual strongly desires promotion as an outcome (valence) he will perform well if he thinks that in so doing there is a high probablity that the organization will actually reward him with promotion (expectancy).

It should be evident why expectancy theory is viewed in terms of a **contingency approach** – people will act in different ways as they seek differing outcomes and in accordance with their perception of the relationship between performance and outcome.

Vroom's expectancy theory has been further developed by Porter and Lawler (1968) who include a number of refinements. These are as follows:

1. An additional expectancy has to be included since there is no guarantee that a person who attempts to perform in a certain way will actually succeed. In their model this is called expectancy type I which is an **effort/performance probability** (E-P), i.e. the probability that effort will lead to successful performance.

2. Vroom's original expectancy becomes expectancy type II, the **performance/outcome probability** (P-O), i.e. the probability of performance leading to a particular outcome.

3. In translating effort into successful performance two further factors have to be considered: the *individual's ability* and his *role perception*. Role perception is how well the individual understands his position relative to the situation he finds himself in, and ability is his competence to perform the task and achieve the outcome.

4. Vroom's model did not consider the contents of outcomes. Rather, these were left to individual choice. However, Porter and Lawler do discuss some of the content of the rewards people may contemplate. Hence in their model they differentiate between *intrinsic* and *extrinsic* rewards (or outcomes) which resemble Maslow's higher and lower order needs.

5. Whether or not the individual is satisfied with the reward, which will of course influence his future valences, depends on the individual's perception of *equity* or fairness. If the reward is seen as being fair then the individual will be satisfied.

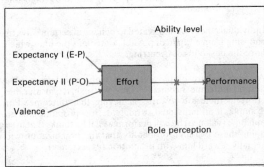

Figure 24. The Porter and Lawler expectancy model. (Points 1–3)

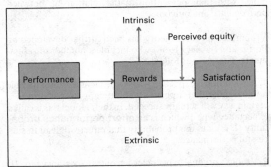

Figure 25. The Porter and Lawler expectancy model. (Points 4–6)

6. Porter and Lawler also dispute the proposition that if managers can improve job satisfaction then increased productivity will follow. The Human Relations School and subsequent behavioral scientists argued that positive work attitudes in terms of job satisfaction had a marked effect in improving job performance. The causal relationship between satisfaction and performance has been the focus for a number of research studies. Vroom concludes from his research that labor turnover, and to a lesser degree absenteeism, is negatively related to job satisfaction. However, Vroom discovered that the statistical relationship between job satisfaction and performance was not significant. Porter and Lawler *reverse* the cause and effect relationship arguing that good performance which elicits rewards causes job satisfaction. The direction of causation has attracted some controversy with numerous empirical studies providing conflicting evidence. Another possible alternative is that satisfaction and performance are both caused by additional variables, especially rewards. The Porter and Lawler relationship is illustrated in Figures 24 and 25.

Expectancy theory has been criticized for being far too rational – do people actually go through the process of weighing up expectancies and placing values on the attractiveness of outcomes? This is difficult to test empirically.

Theorist	Models of man	Contribution
Scientific management (Taylor)	Economic man	Man primarily motivated by financial reward
Human Relations School (Mayo)	Social man	Importance of informal organizations on human behavior
Maslow	Self-actualizing man	Hierarchy of needs
Herzberg	Self-actualizing man	Motivation-hygiene theory
McGregor	Self-actualizing man	Theory X, Theory Y views of man
Vroom	Complex man (Contingency view)	Expectancy theory

Figure 26. Major contributors to theories of motivation

Furthermore, the implications for management are probably not as easily discernible as those of Herzberg, though,
like Herzberg, expectancy theorists emphasize the link between work motivation and the design of jobs. They also
highlight the importance of intrinsic rewards, although their
theory of motivation does not preclude individuals having a
higher valence for the extrinsic rewards.

SUMMARY

This chapter differentiated theories of motivation into two
groups – content and process theories. The former addresses the question of *what* motivates while the latter examines
the *processes* through which people are motivated. Allied to
these theories of motivation were basic managerial assumptions about the nature of man, and the approaches of
economic man, social man, self-actualizing man and complex man were outlined in turn. Figure 26 is a brief summary
of the major contributors to theories of motivation. Reference has been made to two implications of motivation
theories – job design and payment systems. Chapter 10
examines leadership, another area where theories of motivation are applicable.

Influence, Power, Authority, Leadership

INTRODUCTION

The discussion of goals in Chapter 2 referred to the fact that individuals have goals which are not always in line with those of the organization. Chapter 9 demonstrated how people possessing a similar ability level may perform differently due to motivational factors and examined what motivates people (content theories) and how people are motivated (process theories). Based on this understanding of the complexity of individual motivation, managers, acting as leaders, have to motivate employees so that they channel their efforts into pursuing organization goals. **Leadership** forms the bridge between organization goals and individual goals and is a crucial element in determining the success of the organization. It is the process by which managers *influence* the behavior and attitudes of subordinates.

How can managers become more effective leaders? The answer to this question is important to organizations seeking to improve their performance and also has implications for the selection and training of managers. Before attempting to answer this question, the first part of this chapter will look at authority, power and influence in organizations, all of which are inextricably linked to the leadership process. The effectiveness of leadership, as shall be seen later, is related in part to the leader's power base.

INFLUENCE, POWER AND AUTHORITY IN ORGANIZATIONS

Human relations in organizations are concerned with the interaction of individuals and groups, and behind this interaction usually lies power and influence as the efforts of employees are steered towards the goals of the organization. Many writers have stated that fundamental to an understanding of behavior in organizations is an understanding of the nature of influence, power and authority. What then are influence, power and authority?

Influence is where A (the influencer) changes the attitudes or behavior of B (the influencee). **Power** is interpreted as the capability to exercise influence over the behavior of others and is often defined in Dahl's terms (1957) as being something A has over B, to the extent that A can get B to act in a certain way, a way in which B may not have acted but for the power that A had over B. The more power individuals or groups have, the more successful they are likely to be in influencing the attitudes and behavior of other individuals and groups. Though closely associated with power, **authority** is distinguished as the *right* to influence and is equivalent to legitimate power.

Most organizations are of a hierarchical nature and the chain of command is downwards through the hierarchy. At different levels in the hierarchy, authority will be exercised by someone performing a role, e.g. a foreman, a plant manager. The degree of influence attached to a role will depend on its level in the hierarchy – the higher the level the greater the degree of influence. The authority or right to issue commands is viewed as legitimate because it is accepted by the members of the organization as residing in the position the person in authority occupies in the hierarchy. Weber called this kind of authority **rational-legal authority**. He also identified two other types of authority – **charismatic authority**, which is respected by organization members because of the person's qualities, and **traditional authority**, which results from well-established methods of operating within the organization.

Rational-legal authority is dependent upon an organization's acceptance of its legitimacy but in the post-war period most industrially developed countries have experienced major challenges to legitimate authority in many of their major institutions. Rising education levels and higher standards of living have contributed to higher expectations concerning work, with employees wanting greater influence over the decisions taken in organizations to which they belong. The major challenge to managerial authority has come from trade unions, who have sought to reduce the decision-making areas over which management has sole control. (The unilateral rights of management to make rules which influence the employment relationship is sometimes referred to as **managerial prerogative**.) As a result there has been an extension in the scope of collective bargaining and joint consultation, increasing demands for more interesting work and for employee representation on boards of directors.

A number of countries in Western Europe already have some form of employee representation on company boards of directors, for example, the West German co-determination system. The EEC legal harmonization program is likely to extend board representation regulations to all member states. In the UK the public sector has initiated a number of experiments; for example, since 1968 the British Steel Corporation has had worker directors on its divisional boards.

The process of **collective bargaining** itself is a power relationship between organized labor and management and illustrates that power is not exclusively in the hands of management. It is a process which seeks to resolve the conflict of interest which may exist between the management and the work force. Where management has recognized trade unions as being a legitimate interest group within the organization, trade unions in turn have recognized the legitimacy of management to manage within the agreed constraints established by collective bargaining.

Further power relationships that have drawn attention in the past years are consumer groups. Their ability to stimulate the awareness of people and to mobilize them in boycott actions, for instance, has been quite prominent. Management has to recognize different stakeholders; it must heed their requirements at least to some extent.

The manager's "right to manage" is likely to be challenged further in the future. As well as being constrained by workers' organizations, managerial authority is increasingly restricted by legislation introduced by governments, for example, unfair dismissal rights, social responsibilities in terms of the environment.

The above discussion has briefly explored the challenges to managerial authority which may be equated with **legitimate power**. However, other sources of power may be open to managers and an examination of these alternatives helps us to understand how individuals are capable of influencing other people. French and Raven (1959) identified five bases of individual power. Taking A as the influencer and B as the influencee, these are as follows:

1. Position power or **legitimate power** This is the power which is based upon the formal rights and duties attached to a role in the organization hierarchy. The influence of A is considered legitimate and is accepted by B. The rights of the role include the right to information which may come from above or below that organization level, the right of access to organization decision-making bodies, for example, committees, and the right to organize work activities. With this power source, individuals tend to influence other individuals or groups by *rules* and *procedures* which may restrict individual freedom or maintain the status quo. For these rules and procedures to have the desired effect on B, A's right to make the rules and procedures must be accepted by B and A must normally have the resource power to back up his position power; this leads on to the second major power base.

2. Resource power or **reward power** The validity of position power normally requires the backup of resource power which is the control A has over rewards to B. To be effective B must obviously value the rewards which A has under his control. The most obvious rewards over which A has control and B values are financial rewards, for example, pay and fringe benefits. However, rewards may not just be financial and may include status and recognition. Resource power is usually mediated via *exchange* or *bargaining methods* where A gives B something for behaving in the way A requires. The effort-bargain relationship common to pay bargaining agreements, especially where payment by results schemes operate, is a good example of this method of influence in that workers will exert an amount of effort in return for certain financial rewards.

3. Coercive power This is also closely related to resource power and is the power to decide not to reward and to punish non-obedience: the ability of A to punish B. Punishment in industrial organizations is not of course of a physical nature, but can, for example, include such measures as demotion, withholding salary increases, transfer to other work and dismissal. The method of influence implied is one of *force*, though again in industrial organizations this is rarely, if ever, physical force. However, in the collective bargaining relationship a coercive approach to *persuade* the other side to agree to your offer or claim may entail the use of economic force, where each side has the power to inflict economic damage on their opponent. A strike or lock-out would involve the loss of wages to individual workers and the loss of company profits.

4. Expert power Challenges to managerial authority have tended to be directed towards the previous three sources of power, whereas the remaining power bases appear to be more acceptable. Expert power stems from A having the knowledge and skill in an area which B does not possess; therefore in this area B is willing to accept A's influence. A can usually obtain B's compliance by persuasion. Expert power in areas which are crucial to the attainment of organization success may give the powerholder an important organization role with its associated position power source. So, if A's expertise is questioned it may be possible for A to resort to the methods associated with position power or resource power. The level of expert power exercised will be related to the degree to which A can be substituted. If A is difficult to replace he is likely to be in a very strong position.

5. Personal power or **referent power** This is similar to Weber's charismatic authority type. A's power stems from his personal attributes and B will accept A's influence because he admires him. A may try to influence B through persuasion, which is facilitated by personal power, but often the charisma of A alone will be sufficient to get B to alter his behavior. It is worth noting that the method of *persuasion* can be used with any power source and though time-consuming it is normally a very acceptable method – individuals feel that they are doing something for the power holder to which they have voluntarily given their consent.

Having defined the purpose of **leadership** in terms of influencing the behavior and attitudes of other people, the effectiveness of a leader must depend to some extent on power. The leader has to understand his sources of power and the methods of influence he can utilize. It is also important to realize that within organizations numerous individuals and groups have some modicum of power, if not quite considerable power. Power therefore is **relative** and the amount of successful influence an individual may have will depend on how far the balance of power is "tilted" in his favor. In a similar vein the manager may not be the only leader in the organization; for example, leaders emerge from work groups, trade unionists elect shop stewards, Etzioni (1964) makes a useful distinction between formal and informal leaders. An **informal leader** controls others by using mainly personal power. A **formal leader** controls others by using both position power and personal power and it is within this category that managers fall. Against this background, the next section of this chapter deals with theories which seek to answer the question: how can managers become more effective leaders?

LEADERSHIP THEORIES

Leadership is a vital part in the control system within an organization since it is the major process by which managers influence the attitudes and behavior of their subordinates. Theories on leadership fall into three categories:

1. Trait Theory.
2. Style Theory.
3. Contingency Theory or Interaction Approach.

Trait Theory

Sometimes referred to as the "great man" theory, this theory argues that leaders emerge and are effective because they possess certain **personality traits**, for example, intelligence, self-confidence, extroversion, maturity, decisiveness. This again is associated with Weber's charismatic type of authority and people in leadership, because of their personality, are usually described as having a certain charisma.

Empirical studies, however, indicate that there is little correlation between personality characteristics and success as a leader. The possession of certain personality characteristics alone cannot determine a good or bad leader. This does not mean to say that anyone can become a leader; to understand what makes a leader effective, the circumstances of the situation must be taken into account. The trend has been away from trait theory to the study of the interaction between different styles of leadership and different situations. Before looking at the interaction approach consideration must be given to style theories.

Style Theory

Instead of concentrating on the leader's personality, style theory concentrates on the **behavior patterns** of the leader. Is one leadership style preferable to another? If so, what should this style be? Research on leadership style has been developed by the Human Relations and Neo-Human Relations Schools who saw leaders as being important in the promotion of job satisfaction and organization efficiency.

The earliest studies on style were carried out by Lewin *et al.* (1939) who organized twenty boys into four clubs to undertake a task and subjected them to three different styles of leadership (illustrated in Figure 27).

1. Autocratic What has to be done and how the task will be carried out is determined solely by the leader. His relationship with subordinates is mainly directional, namely the issuing of orders.

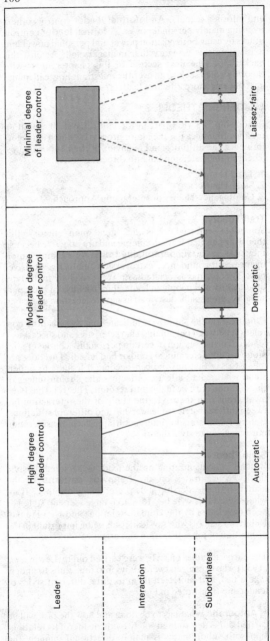

Figure 27. Leadership styles

2. Democratic Decisions on what has to be done and how the task should be carried out are taken after group discussion – a participative approach. Leader relationship with subordinates is supportive giving guidance to group members when required.

3. Laissez-faire involves little external leader interference in the form of guidance or providing encouragement. Group members work largely unsupported and the leader's role is similar to that of other group members.

The results of the experiment showed that though the productivity of the group under autocratic leadership was highest it tended to decline when the leader was not present. Under democratic leadership productivity was still fairly high – not significantly different from the group supervised by autocratic leadership – but performance was maintained when the leader was absent and quality was better. It was also the style which was most popular among the boys and offered greatest task satisfaction. On most counts the laissez-faire style produced very poor results.

This began the wave of thinking that the **democratic style** of leadership was the best style to pursue but, since this study in 1939, further research projects have attempted to discover more precisely the relationship between leadership style and employee performance. Most of these studies, though using different terms, still differentiated style according to the autocratic-democratic distinction.

McGregor's Theory X and Theory Y, which outline managerial assumptions on the nature of man, have been examined in Chapter 9. Clearly they have an impact on the leadership style exercised by the manager. A manager acting on Theory X assumptions is likely to be autocratic whereas Theory Y managers are likely to be democratic. Concerning the motivation of employees, it is also evident that the autocratic style basically aims at meeting lower order needs, and employees heavily concerned with security seem to be reasonably satisfied under this style. In contrast, the democratic style of Theory Y, as illustrated by management by objectives (see Chapter 4), seeks to move towards meeting the employees' higher order needs by delegating responsibility and control downwards to the individual or the group.

The Survey Research Center at the University of Michigan (1950s and 1960s) examined differences in supervisory styles applied to low producing and high producing groups of employees. These experiments covered a range of work environments from insurance companies through to railway maintenance teams. Supervisory style was classified as **employee-centered** which corresponded to the democratic style of management, and **production-centered** which corresponded to a more authoritarian style of management. The results showed that higher producing groups were supervised in an employee-centered manner and workers in such groups experienced higher job satisfaction than their counterparts operating under production-centered supervision.

Although seen originally as a continuum of leadership effectiveness this classification was later viewed as two dimensional: in other words, supervisors could be both employee-centered and production-centered to varying degrees. This finding is similar to that obtained by the Ohio State University Studies which highlighted two independent dimensions as being significant to leadership effectiveness.

1. Initiating structure This is where the supervisor or manager organizes the work to be done by defining roles, assigning tasks, planning and generally controlling what has to be done.

2. Consideration This is the amount of consideration the supervisor gives to his subordinates and reflects his respect for them, and the mutual trust and friendship between them. Thus, this dimension usually involves participative decision-making and a two-way flow of communication.

Supervisors may, of course, exhibit varying degrees of dimensions 1 and 2, and Fleishmann and Harris (1962) analyzed the relationship between these dimensions and **employee morale** (measured by the rate of labor turnover and number of employee grievances). Both these indirect measures of employee morale were in line with other studies; morale was good when supervisory style was high in consideration and the reverse when consideration was low.

Still in a similar vein, Blake and Mouton's studies (1961) established a **managerial grid** which was a simple presentation combining the two significant dimensions of leadership style. In their style classification, *concern for people* formed the Y axis and *concern for production* the X axis. Each dimension was measured on a scale of 1 to 9 in terms of the extent of its presence in the manager's leadership style. The style they advocated as being ideal was the **9 : 9 style**, that is a manager who scores high on concern for people and high on concern for production. Based on a questionnaire managers could identify where they lay on the graph in terms of style and then, through a training program, be encouraged to move towards adopting a 9 : 9 style.

It is worth mentioning here Likert's systems of management. The work of Likert at Michigan University, which was based on extensive research, concluded that there are four recognizable systems of management. Likert's systems of management are broader than the individual leadership style approach since they focus upon the operating procedures and actions which dominate management in the entire organization. Hence, the system of management is seen as establishing the organization climate and includes structure, communications, leadership, motivation, decision-making procedures, evaluation and interpersonal relations. A continuum approach is again adopted and to fit organizations on to the continuum their profiles are determined by a questionnaire administered to managers.

The four management systems identified by Likert are as follows:

System 1: Exploitive – authoritative
Decisions are taken at the top of the hierarchical structure; there is tight authoritarian control over performance and coercive power may be used.

System 2: Benevolent – authoritative
Again decisions are taken at the top of the hierarchical structure but, in return for their loyalty, employees will be treated reasonably well and in a rather paternalistic manner.

System 3: Consultative
Management retains the right to take all decisions but discusses common problems with its employees. The atmosphere is more one of cooperation and there is a two-way exchange of information.

System 4: Participative – group
More participative in terms of employee involvement in management decisions than System 3. Mutual trust develops between employees and management. Decisions are often taken by group decision-making processes and supervision is supportive rather than authoritative.

Likert's "ideal" system for organization effectiveness is System 4.

Having summarized the major contributors to the style approach to leadership effectiveness, what conclusions can be drawn? Most of the studies put forward by style theorists seem to indicate that the democratic style of leadership is the best style for managers to adopt since it tends to improve organization performance. Note that the "democratic" dimension is common to most style theories although terminology may vary (illustrated in Figure 28). Current theorists take more account of the **situational variables** which may determine whether or not a particular leadership style is effective in a certain set of circumstances – a **best fit** approach where style is fitted to the situation rather than merely a **best style** approach undertaken irrespective of the situation. This approach is further reinforced by other research studies which produce less convincing evidence in favor of the supportive or democratic style of management.

Clearly, as the studies already mentioned illustrate, there are numerous situations where democratic styles of leadership are associated with higher performance levels and higher levels of job satisfaction. However, other studies have shown that in repetitive routine work the production oriented leader promotes higher productivity. Secondly, some workers may prefer to be directed in an

SOURCE OF RESEARCH	AUTOCRATIC	DEMOCRATIC
McGregor	Theory X	Theory Y
Ohio State University	Initiating structure	Consideration
Michigan University	Production centered	Employee centered
Likert	System 1	System 4
Blake and Mouton	Grid reference 9:1 Task management	Grid reference 9:9 Team management
Fiedler	Task oriented Low LPC	Relationship oriented High LPC
Tannenbaum and Schmidt	Boss centered leadership	Subordinate centered leadership

Figure 28. Terminology used in describing leadership styles

authoritative fashion. Vroom and Mann (1960) showed that the degree of interaction between supervisor and subordinate may influence employee attitudes towards the leader. Where superior-subordinate interaction was limited, the latter had a more positive attitude towards an authoritarian style of supervision, while, in situations where interaction was considerable, employees had a more positive attitude towards participative leaders. Personality factors of the subordinate may also be important; for example, individuals with a low need for independence or who are authoritarian themselves may not link their satisfaction to the degree of participation in decision-making. Thirdly, there are studies which question the nature of the cause and effect relationship between the supervisory style adopted and the level of employee performance. In other words, high levels of employee satisfaction and performance may evoke participative behavior from supervisors. Fourthly, in practice it is difficult to isolate the effect of supervisory style on performance since other variables in the situation may be operating to increase performance levels; for example, an incentive payment scheme may be contributing to improved performance as well as a democratic style of leadership. For this reason, experimental studies in laboratories have been carried out and though of questionable validity the evidence produced from a number of these studies was not conclusively in favor of the best style viewpoint.

It would appear then, that there is sufficient doubt from studies of the effectiveness of the best style approach to indicate that closer attention must be given to the situational variables. The interaction or contingency approach takes account not only of style but also of other variables contributing to the context in which the leader finds himself.

Contingency theory or interaction approach

The work of Fiedler (1967) was one of the first major contributions to the development of the contingency view of leadership. Before defining those situational variables he thought were significant, Fiedler distinguished between leadership styles according to two dimensions which are somewhat similar to those previously derived by style theorists. A leader could place his style on a continuum varying between a controlling, structuring style to that of a considerate, participative style. His position would be determined by his score on a questionnaire designed to discover the leader's opinions on the person he least preferred in the work group—**the least preferred co-worker** (LPC) (Figure 29).

Fiedler detected from his research studies on leadership that leaders with a high LPC or a low LPC were correlated with successful performance; hence no one LPC was correlated with success. Therefore, style was not the only variable which determined effectiveness but had to be taken into account along with the combination of three other situational variables, which were:

1. Leader-member relations Leader acceptability by the

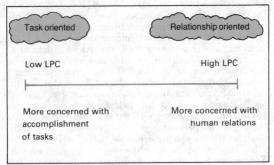

Figure 29. Fiedler's leadership styles

group, measured as good or poor.

2. Task structure Degree to which the task was well defined, measured as structured or unstructured.

3. Leader position power Legitimate power given to the leader by the organization or group, measured as strong or weak.

The leader's situation was, therefore, categorized by these three variables which combined to give varying degrees of **favorability** or **unfavorability**. The combination for a favorable situation for the leader was one where the leader-member relationship was good, the task was highly structured and the leader's position power was strong. Conversely, an unfavorable situation was marked by poor leader-member relations, and unstructured task and weak leader-position power. Between these extremes were six other possible situations yielding varying degrees of favorability and unfavorability.

From experimental results, Fiedler concluded that in favorable and unfavorable situations leaders whose style was **task oriented** (low LPC) were more suitable. However, in moderately favorable situations (for example, where leader-member relations were good, the task was unstructured and leader position power was weak) **relationship oriented** leaders were more suitable.

The trend in research is increasingly one of identifying the situational variables and showing how they interact with style to optimize leader effectiveness. Indeed, Fiedler has been criticized for underestimating the complexity of the leadership situation while his LPC scores have been questioned on the grounds of reliability and validity. Clearly then, to understand what makes a good leader (in terms of employee performance) the manager must consider, as indicated by Tannenbaum and Schmidt, factors related to the leader himself, his subordinates and the situation in which the leader finds himself.

Tannenbaum and Schmidt (1958), like other writers, first attempted to classify styles on the decision-making continuum (illustrated in Figure 30). (Note the similarities with the other approaches described above.)

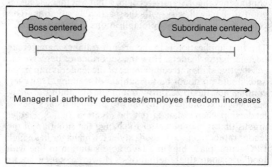

Figure 30. Tannenbaum and Schmidt's leadership styles

The style adopted by a manager is a function of:

1. Factors influencing the leader's choice of style, for example, his value system, confidence, risk profile.

2. Factors influencing the subordinate's choice of style, for example, independent needs, tolerance of ambiguity, task interest, knowledge and experience.

3. Factors influencing the situation, for example, organization characteristics, task characteristics, work group characteristics.

The position the leader occupies on the scale will therefore depend on the "push" and "pull" of the three factors described above.

Tannenbaum and Schmidt's analysis of the situational variables has been developed by other writers. For example, Handy (1976) substitutes the third situational variable with task characteristics and adds a fourth factor, the environment in which the interaction of the leaders, the subordinates and the task takes place. In the environment factor, he includes Fiedler's position power and leader-member relations, and adds organization norms, structure and technology, and the variety of tasks and subordinates. Therefore, to be effective, managers have to be aware of the numerous constraints placed upon the style they adopt and must be prepared to adjust their style as variables change over time.

CONCLUSION ON LEADERSHIP

At the beginning of this chapter the question which was asked was how could managers become more effective leaders? Despite years of research, mentioned briefly above, this question cannot be answered conclusively.

However, the current view tends to emphasize the interaction of variables related to the leader himself, his subordinates and the situation. Previous theorists concentrated on personality traits and the behavioral style of the leader but contingency theorists now recognize that whether a leader is good or bad will vary with the particular situation. This conclusion has a number of implications for management.

The first implication is in the area of training managers to become better leaders. How the subordinates perceive the substantive skills and competence of the leader is important and should no doubt be the subject of training. However, contingency theorists throw doubt on the ability of management development programs to produce ideal styles of leadership when isolated from the situation. In fact, Fiedler argues that it may be easier to change the situation of the leader rather than the leader's style: if a manager has a high LPC score, place him in a favorable situation in line with Fiedler's contextual definitions. However, taken to its extreme this might exclude any leadership training. In many cases it is probably still easier to attempt to develop the skills of the leader to enable him to meet the needs of the situation rather than to change the situation. Managers should be trained to identify their style of management and to adapt to their situation or else try to ensure, where possible, that they are placed in the situation which most closely matches their style.

In the United Kingdom an influential leadership training program was devised by Adair *et al.* called **Action Centered Leadership** (ACL). Originally devised for developing leadership qualities in army officer cadets, it has been adapted for application in various types of industrial organizations. The essence of the program is to develop those activities which a leader undertakes; hence the emphasis is on the actions the leader performs. Since these actions comprise the functions of leadership it is sometimes referred to as **functional leadership**. While accepting that the qualities of the leader have to be matched to the situation, this approach sees the leader performing his functions in order to meet three interrelated need areas: *individual needs, group needs* and the *needs to accomplish the task*. The specific leadership functions required to accommodate all these needs may vary with the situation, although Adair (1973) lists a number of functions which may be generally applicable. These include planning, initiating, controlling, supporting, informing and evaluating. In a similar vein other writers, notably Shipman (1968), have discussed leadership patterns in terms of instrumental, expressive and moral requirements. The concern of the instrumental leader is to complete the task at hand but with a concomitant likelihood of increasing group hostility and alienation. Conversely the expressive leader tends to be concerned both with the group as a cohesive unit and with the development and maturation of the individuals within that group. The expressive leader is more likely to resort to rewards rather than to punishment in order to encourage the group members and to maintain some semblance of order and discipline.

The second implication, from our understanding of leadership effectiveness, affects the **selection** of managers or the spotting of potential promotees. The selection process often stresses the personality traits of managers but it has been discovered that no one set of personality traits corresponds to successful leadership. To meet the various situational needs present in industrial organizations, different personalities and leadership styles will be required on the part of managers. Therefore, selection panels and promotion boards must balance their findings on personality traits with information on other situational factors; for example, if the situation requires a considerate leader, how good is the applicant in exercising interpersonal skills?

While recognizing that the contingency or interaction approach has improved our understanding of the role of the manager as an effective leader, it should be remembered that, though of great importance, organization success will also depend on other factors besides leadership, for example the organization structure, technology, expertise, product markets.

SUMMARY

The first part of the chapter was designed to provide the setting for the study of leadership and dealt with authority, power and influence: all fundamental to an understanding of the interaction between individuals and groups in organizations. Weber's charismatic, traditional and rational-legal authority types were identified and the alternative sources of power and methods of influence outlined. The chapter then went on to investigate various approaches to improving our understanding of the factors contributing to effective leadership. Three approaches were studied in some depth: trait theory, style theory and contingency theory. It was concluded that a contingency approach which seeks to match style to the working environment is the most useful way of improving our understanding of effective leadership.

Further Reading

Adair, J., *Action-Centered Leadership* (McGraw-Hill, 1973)

Blake, R.R., Mouton, J.S., *The Managerial Grid* (Gulf, 1964)

Blau, P.M. and Scott, W.R., *Formal Organizations: a comparative approach* (Routledge & Kegan Paul, 1963)

Burns, T. and Stalker, G.M., *The Management of Innovation* (Tavistock, 1961)

Chandler, A.D. Jr., *Strategy and Structure* (Doubleday & Co., 1966)

Child, J., *Organization, A guide to problems and practice* (Harper & Row, 1977)

Cyert, R.M. and March, J.G., *A Behavioral Theory of the Firm* (Prentice-Hall, 1963)

Etzioni, A., *The Comparative Analysis of Complex Organizations* (Free Press, 1961)

Fiedler, F.E., *A Theory of Leadership Effectiveness* (McGraw-Hill, 1967)

Galbraith, J., *Organization Design* (Addison Wesley, 1977)

Herzberg, F., *Work and the Nature of Man* (Staples Press, 1968)

Katz, D. and Kahn, R.L., *The Social Psychology of Organization* (Wiley, second edition, 1978)

Likert, R., *The Human Organization: Its Management and Value* (McGraw-Hill, 1967)

Lupton, T., *Management and the Social Sciences* (Penguin, second edition, 1971)

March, J.G. and Simon, H.A., *Organizations* (Wiley, 1958)

Maslow, A.H., *Motivation and Personality* (Harper & Row, 1954)

McClelland, D.C., *The Achieving Society* (Van Nostrand Reinhold, 1961)

McGregor, D., *The Human Side of Enterprise* (McGraw-Hill, 1960)

Ouchi, W.G., *Theory Z* (Addison Wesley, 1981)

Perrow, C., *Complex Organizations – A Critical Essay* (Scott Foresman, 1979)

Pfeffer, J., *Power in Organizations* (Pitman, 1981)

Porter, L.W. and Lawler, E.E., *Managerial Attitudes and Performance* (Dorsey-Irwin, 1968)

Porter, M.E., *Competitive Strategies* (Free Press, 1981)

Sayles, L.R., *The Behavior of Industrial Work Groups* (Wiley, 1958)

Schein, E.H., *Organizational Psychology* (Prentice-Hall, 1965)

Silverman, D., *The Theory of Organizations* (Basic Books, 1971)

Thompson, J.D., *Organizations in action: social science bases of administrative theory* (McGraw-Hill, 1967)

Weick, K.E., *The Social Psychology of Organizing* (Addison Wesley, 1979)

Woodward, J., *Industrial Organization: Theory and Practice* (Oxford University Press, 1965)

Glossary

Achievement motivation The drive of individuals to achieve their goals. McClelland classified individuals as being either low or high achievers.

Alienation Non-identification with or estrangement from the organization, its values and purposes. The cog-in-the-machine-feeling divorces man from his own nature.

Attitude A definite opinion which manifests itself in the evaluation of ideas, objects or persons on a favorable or unfavorable basis.

Authority The right to influence other individuals or groups.

Autocratic A leadership style, sometimes called authoritarian, where the leader dictates the planning and execution of tasks with little or no participation from subordinates.

Autonomous work groups Associated with the socio-technical systems school of thought, where groups of workers are given considerable autonomy and control over a complete unit of work which enables them to be responsible for planning, organizing, coordinating, executing and evaluating their work.

Behavioral theory of organization goals Based on the work of Cyert and March who argue that an organization has multiple goals since it is a coalition of different interest groups each of whom pursue their own set of goals and can influence managerial decision-making.

Bureaucracy An organization (first described in the writings of Weber) whose characteristics include stability, a high degree of centralized control and a closed system approach to problem solving.

Business concerns A category of Blau and Scott's classification of organizations where the primary beneficiaries are the owners of the organization.

Causal texture Effects of the relationship and interaction between different parts of the environment, and their impact on the organization.

Centralization Concentration of authority and responsibility at the top of the organization hierarchy.

Chain of command Offices which comprise the various levels of officially defined authority and responsibility.

Charismatic authority Authority which is accepted by members of the organization due to the personal qualities (charisma) of the authority holder.

Classical Organization Theory The collective term used to describe theories on organizations developed in the early half of this century. It contains three major strands – scientific management, formal organization theory and bureaucracy. All these theories concentrated on formal organization structure and assumed man behaved in a rational economic manner.

Coercive organizations A category of Etzioni's classification of organizations where members of the organization have a low level of commitment to organization goals and their involvement is described as alienative, e.g. prisons.

Coercive power The ability of an individual to punish another individual.

Cognitive The process of understanding and acquiring knowledge.

Cognitive dissonance A state of mind experienced by an individual whose perceptions regarding related objects, events, circumstances and knowledge are out of balance with each other.

Commonweal organizations A category of Blau and Scott's classification of organizations where the primary beneficiary is the general public, e.g. police force.

Complex man view A view of man developed by Schein, which is a reaction to the simplistic generalizations of alternative views of man and emphasizes the differences in individual motives and the fact that there is not necessarily a single strategy for managing people that is applicable in all situations.

Conflict Disagreement arising from opposite viewpoints, leading to loss of efficiency and/or effectiveness.

Consonance A state of agreement or harmony existing between viewpoints, factors and influences of the individual.

Content theories of motivation Theories which examine the nature of individual needs which cause people to act in certain ways.

Contingency Theory A theory which argues that optimal solutions to organization problems are derived from matching the internal organization structures and processes to their external environment.

Corporate planning Translation of strategy into tasks – how and when it will be achieved.

Decentralization Delegation of authority and responsibility to lower levels within an organization structure.

Democratic A leadership style where the leader allows a degree of group participation in decision-making. Note the degree of participation may vary, for example, with the level and content of decisions.

Deviant behavior Behavior which does not accord to some established norm.

Differentiation Differences between parts of the organization and/or environment.

Divisional structure Name given to a structure built around recognizable parts of the company's business, and where such parts have considerable autonomy, authority and responsibility.

Dominant competitive issue The major environmental influence acting on industry/organization, e.g. product innovation.

Dysfunction Unanticipated and undesirable consequences arising, for example, as the result of a particular decision.

Economic man A view of man which considers financial rewards as the primary motivator of individuals at work.

Effectiveness A measure of how successful an organization is in attaining its goals and functioning as a social unit.

Efficiency A measure of how well an organization has utilized its resources in attaining its goals.

Empirical Evidence accruing as a result of experimentation and observation.

Enactment Active role taken by the individual in defining his environment by interpreting it and by acting on the basis of this interpretation.

Expectancy Theory of Motivation A theory which takes account not only of the outcomes people value from acting in a certain way, but also their expectations that action will lead to the desired outcome. Vroom's Expectancy Theory states that motivation (F) is a function of the expectancy (E) and the valence (V): $F = f(E \times V)$.

Expert power Power which is based on a person's specialist knowledge and skills.

External environment Any activity or source of influence outside the organization.

Extrinsic motivation Motivation resulting from factors external to the individual.

Feedback Consequences of actions or decisions communicated to the originator.

Festinger American psychologist concerned with development of cognitive theory and, in particular, cognitive dissonance.

Formal authority Official authority conferred on units, e.g. individuals, departments, by virtue of office held or function performed.

Formal communication Providing information to whoever the official organization determines.

Formal groups A group of people established to fulfil official organization goals.

Formal leader A leader who has been appointed and exercises control over others through legitimate and personal power.

Formal Organization Theory The term used to describe the writings of managerial practitioners, e.g. Fayol, Gulick, Urwick, who developed principles for organization structure and management. These included the scalar principle, the concept of unity of command, functional specialization, spans of control and minimum authority levels.

Framework of reference Parameters which define the limits surrounding the formation of views, attitudes and activity.

Functional structure A pattern of components and relationships built around the major, specialized activities of a business.

Gestalt The organized whole, made up of the individual parts, but which is greater than their sum.

Goal displacement This occurs when an organization's original goals are substituted by other goals which normally represent the means to achieve those original goals.

Group dynamics Processes of interaction (synergy) among group members which facilitate its operations.

Group norm A common viewpoint or standard to which all members are expected to subscribe.

Hawthorne experiments A series of experiments conducted in the 1920s and early 1930s at the Hawthorne Works of the Western Electric Company of Chicago by Mayo and associates. Experiments, designed to measure the effects on productivity after various working conditions were altered (e.g. illumination levels, rest pauses and incentives), revealed that irrespective of changing conditions, output increased. This was considered the result of more social intercourse between workers, researchers and supervisors and this general conclusion highlighted the importance of social factors at work.

Hierarchy Organization where posts are graded according to level of authority and responsibility.

Higher order needs Needs which appear at the upper levels of Maslow's hierarchy – self-actualization and esteem. These are closely related to Herzberg's motivator factors (see **Motivation-Hygiene Theory**) and McGregor's **Theory Y** view (see below).

Holistic A fully developed and embracing viewpoint, e.g. towards the organization's objectives.

Homogeneous environment All parts of the environment (sub-environments) working uniformly.

Human Relations School A school of thought developed from the Hawthorne experiments conducted in the 1930s. It emphasizes the social factors influencing behavior at work, highlighting the importance of aspects like interpersonal relations, leadership styles, communications, employee morale and job satisfaction.

Influence Where A (the influencer) changes the attitudes or behavior of B (the influencee).

Informal groups Individuals who act collectively on the basis of friendship or shared interests.

Informal leader A leader who has been voluntarily accepted by others, and exercises control through personal power.

Information processing perspective Organizations are viewed as continually engaged in making decisions. The organizational structure should be designed to optimize flow of information. By making information available, uncertainty can be reduced and decisions can be made.

Instrumental orientation The idea that employees are extrinsically motivated at work, primarily by pay and security, and meet their needs outside of the employment situation.

Integration A process of bringing together or ensuring cooperation between different parts of the organization.

Interaction Approach or Contingency Theories of leadership These concentrate on matching leadership style with variables of the situation in which the leader finds himself.

Interlocking directorates Organizations often share one or more directors. The existence of these "interlocks" provides each organization with an increased amount of control over the environment.

Internal environment The organization's culture.

Interpretive paradigm Holds that there is no "objective" view of reality. Experiences are **interpreted** through retrospective sense-making.

Intrinsic motivation Motivation stemming from within the individual.

Intuitive Immediate non-cognitive judgment or formation of opinion.

Job design Relates to consideration of activity specific to the technical requirement and to relationships which enable the job to be performed.

Job enlargement A method of job design, sometimes referred to as horizontal job enlargement, that involves changing the content of a job in order to build in additional tasks which do not require any increase in responsibility levels.

Job enrichment A method of job design, sometimes referred to as vertical job enlargement, that involves changing the content of a job by building in additional tasks which provide greater challenge, responsibility and more opportunity for personal achievement and growth.

Job rotation A method of job design which involves moving workers between jobs usually on some regular time basis so as to introduce some variety into the activities performed by the employee.

Laissez-faire leadership style This is where the leader allows a group of subordinates to work largely autonomously by providing little or no direction or encouragement.

Lateral expansion Widening of hierarchical pyramid, i.e., expansion of number of organization units at similar level.

Legitimate authority Authority which is exercised and accepted on the basis of right attaching to the office and which is distinguished from the use of naked power.

Legitimate power Sometimes referred to as position power: power which is attached to the powerholder's position in the organization hierarchy (see also **Rational-legal authority**).

Likert American group theorist concerned with the role of informal groups within organizations. In *New Patterns of Management*, he proposes an organization structured on the basis of supportive relationships.

Line/staff A structure which consists of line executive and staff advisory functions.

Lower order needs Needs which appear at the lower levels of Maslow's hierarchy – social, safety, physiological. These are closely related to Herzberg's hygiene factors.

Macro-environment The aggregate economic, social, poilitcal, technical cultures.

Management by objectives (M.B.O.) A goal-setting process in which both superiors and subordinates jointly take part.

Management information system Reports on organization performance or standards to which organization members are to adhere.

Managerial grid A grid designed by Blake and Mouton which classifies managerial style as a position on scales of nine points with concern for people on the y axis and concern for production on the x axis. Their favored style was the point 9 : 9, that is, a style high on both concern for people and concern for production.

Maslow's hierarchy of needs A hierarchy that differentiates five need levels and which, in ascending order of relative importance to the individual, are physiological, safety, social, esteem and self-actualization.

Matrix Refers to organizations which embody both traditional and newer approaches to structural design.

Mayo American group therapist who pioneered investigations into social phenomena of work groups – the so-called Hawthorne experiments (see above).

McGregor American social psychologist whose investigations focused on managerial assumptions concerning the nature of human behavior.

Mechanistic organizations Identified by Burns and Stalker as organizations which operate in stable environmental conditions in which decisions are largely of a routine nature. Such organizations are more suited to a rigid, mechanical, beuraucratic type structure.

Motivation The willingness to exert effort in order to achieve a desired outcome or goal which satisfies an individual need.

Motivation-Hygiene Theory Sometimes called Herzberg's Two Factor Theory. A theory which states that job satisfaction and job dissatisfaction are not opposites, but two independent dimensions with the former produced by *motivator factors* (achievement, recognition, work itself, responsibility and advancement) and the latter produced by *hygiene factors* (company policy and administration, supervision, salary, interpersonal relations and working conditions).

Motives The forces underlying human behavior which cause people to behave in certain ways.

Mutual adjustment A process of cooperation and agreement as part of the manager's input–output process between two or more organization units.

Mutual benefit associations A category of Blau and Scott's classification of organizations where the primary beneficiaries are the members of the organization, e.g. trade unions, political parties.

Mutual consensus A process whereby both or all sides in a situation reach agreement as to policies, goals, objectives or procedures.

Neo-Human Relations School A more recent development of the Human Relations School associated with a group of behavioral scientists like Likert, McGregor and Herzberg, who emphasized the importance of intrinsic motivation.

Normative organizations A category of Etzioni's classification of organizations where members of the organization have a high level of commitment to organization goals and their involvement is described as moral, e.g. churches, political parties.

Official goals Goals described by Perrow which represent the formally stated organization goals.

Operative goals Goals described by Perrow which represent the goals which actually influence behavior in organizations and are directly linked to the numerous interest groups which comprise organizations.

Optimum performance Balanced performance in relation to a number of criteria – related to organization effectiveness.

Organic organizations Identified by Burns and Stalker as organizations which operate in a rapidly changing environment and where the need to continually adapt to changing conditions requires a more flexible organization structure.

Organization Where two or more people unite together and coordinate their activities in order to achieve a set of common goals.

Organization goal A future position which an organization plans to achieve.

Organization strategy Official blueprint of an organization's intentions in relation to its objectives.

Path-Goal Approach Individuals choosing the goals they wish to pursue and the paths which will direct them towards their attainment.

Payment by results A wage payment system where an employee's earnings are linked directly to his level of output.

Perception Act of attaching meaning to sensory inputs surrounding external objects, events and circumstances.

Performance The outcome of both the ability and motivation of an individual at work.

Personal power Similar to charismatic authority; this is where the powerholder has the ability to influence others due to their admiration of his personal qualities.

Phenomenological school School of thought holding that there is no objective reality. All perceptions of reality are therefore cognitively constructed. Communication is possible by the existence of shared views and meanings, validated during interactions.

Plurality A number of interests as opposed to one (unitary) interest which all share.

Power The capability of A to exercise influence over the attitudes or behavior of B.

Process theories of motivation Theories which examine the thought processes which individuals undergo before acting in certain ways.

Processes Activities which comprise transformation of inputs into outputs.

Profit centers Definitive parts of the business, e.g. product division with responsibility for profits.

Profit maximization The traditional economist's view of the goal of a business organization.

Project team A number of individuals working together as a unit on a specific project or task.

Psychic Mental/spiritual force or disposition.

Rational-legal authority The equivalent to legitimate power; authority which members of the organization accept as resting in the position which a person occupies in the organization hierarchy.

Reciprocal influence Complementary reaction to an event or activity.

Remunerative organization A category of Etzioni's classification of organizations where members of the organization have a low level of commitment to organization goals and their involvement is described as calculative, for example, business organizations.

Restrictive practices Employee practices which have the effect of reducing output levels and preventing management operating as efficiently and effectively as possible.

Reward power Sometimes referred to as resource power;

this is the ability of an individual to control the rewards which are administered to another individual.

Ringi Form of decision-making. Collective process of decision-making. Proposal regarding a specific problem is issued by lower level management and circulated to all parties affected up to top management. Once the proposal has met approval of everyone involved, it is returned to initiator for implementation.

Role Behavior expected of a person undertaking a particular job.

Role ambiguity Uncertainty surrounding the requirements of a particular role either by the organization or by the individual.

Role conflict Where an individual is faced with incompatible role requirements.

Role overload Where the requirements of role exceed the capabilities of the individual performing it.

Role underload Where the requirements of the role are exceeded by the capabilities of the individual performing it.

Satisficing Suggested by Simon, this is where managers take decisions not to maximize any particular goal but to satisfy the claims of competing interest groups within the organization.

Scalar chain See **Chain of command**.

Scientific management Primarily developed by Taylor, concerned with the application of scientific methods, e.g. work study, to improve the organization of work so as to maximize efficiency.

Self-actualizing man view A view of man which is associated with the Neo-Human Relations School and emphasizes the importance of intrinsic motivation (higher order needs) rather than extrinsic motivation.

Sense-making Under the assumption that there is no objective reality, events are assigned meaning through sense-making.

Service organizations A category of Blau and Scott's classification of organizations where the primary beneficiaries are specific clients drawn from the general public, e.g. universities, hospitals.

Social action theory The organization is viewed as the result of the interlocked behaviors of its members. Individual actions are guided by material constraints and personal interpretations of organizational reality.

Social man view A view of man which is derived from the approach of the Human Relations School, which highlights the importance of social relationships at work, e.g. interpersonal relations, superior-subordinate relationships, group dynamics.

Socio-Technical Systems Approach An approach which views behavior in organizations as a function of both social and technological factors which are independent but also interdependent.

Span of control The number of individuals reporting to any one supervisor or manager.

Standardization A process or control mechanism which enables a predetermined response.

Strategic planning Planning which follows development of the organization's future strategy.

Synergy A process of interaction among individuals which produces a totality, e.g. knowledge, greater than the sum of its parts.

Systems Theory A theory which states that an organization is a system which comprises a number of interdependent component parts which are organized into a whole so that the system is more than simply the sum of its parts.

Sub-environment Any definitive part of the total environment, e.g. technology.

Taylor American engineer and consultant whose views on the management of organizations found expression in his theories of scientific management.

Technocratic Units or personnel who design and/or plan major operational activities.

Technology Important influence on the functioning of organizations highlighted by Woodward's research of manufacturing companies which she classified according to their production technology – unit and small batch, large batch and mass production and process production. She concluded that differences in technology were a major determinant as to the nature of the organization structure, e.g. spans of control, number of authority levels.

Theory X A view of man put forward by McGregor which assumes that man basically dislikes work and responsibility and therefore must be controlled from above on the basis of a reward/punishment psychology.

Theory Y An alternative view of man put forward by McGregor which assumes that man basically likes work and seeks responsibility and is capable of exercising self-direction and self-control at work.

Traditional authority Authority which is accepted by members of the organization as resting with certain individuals because of long established methods of operating within the organization.

Trait Theory A leadership theory which argues that leaders emerge and are effective because of the personal characteristics of the leader.

Turbulent environment An environmental condition characterized by uncertainty and rapid change.

Uncertainty stems from unpredictable chains of events and from excessive complexity. The reduction of uncertainty is the major objective of organizations in the information processing perspective. It is partly accomplished by structuring activities inside the organization, and enhancing control over the environment.

Unitary See **Plurality**.

Valence The preference an individual attaches to a particular outcome resulting from his actions.